C000176988

Textiles Technology

Rose Sinclair • Sue Morgan

Series Editor: Geoff Hancock

www.heinemann.co.uk
✓ Free online support
✓ Useful weblinks
✓ 24 hour online ordering

01865 888058

Heinemann Educational Publishers
Halley Court, Jordan Hill, Oxford, OX2 8EJ
Part of Harcourt Education
Heinemann is the registered trademark of
Harcourt Education Limited

© Harcourt Education, 2006

First published 2006

09 08 07 06 05
10 9 8 7 6 5 4 3 2 1

10-digit ISBN: 0 435413 49 X
13-digit ISBN: 978 0 435413 49 X

British Library Cataloguing in Publication Data is available from the British Library on request

Copyright notice
All rights reserved. No part of this publication may be reproduced in any form or by any means (including photocopying
or storing it in any medium by electronic means and whether or not transiently or incidentally to some other use of this
publication) without the prior written permission of the copyright owner, except in accordance with the provisions of the
Copyright, Designs and Patents Act 1988 or under the terms of a licence issued by the Copyright Licensing Agency Ltd, 90
Tottenham Court Road, London W1T 4LP. Applications for the copyright owner's written permission to reproduce any part of
this publication should be addressed to the publisher.

Designed by Wild Apple Design
Produced by Kamae Design

Printed and bound in the UK by CPIBath

Index compiled by Ian D Crane

Original illustrations © Harcourt Education Limited, 2006

Illustrated by Kamae Design

Photographic acknowledgements
The authors and publisher would like to thank the following for permission to reproduce photographs:
Alamy pp.12, 42 (right), 43, 44, 45, 46(bottom), 61 (bottom left), 62, 72, 74(left), 81, 92, 96 (right), 103, 109; Babylock UK
p.74 (right); Berghaus p.77; Brother pp.96 (left), 98; Cath Kidston p.14 (left); Chris Moore p.94 (right); Corbis pp.9 (bottom),
13 (right), 61 (top left), 66; Environmental images p.38; Excell p.129 (all); Getty pp.13 (left), 82, 95, 108; Harcourt Education/
Susi Paz p.53; Imagebank p.61 (top right); Katharine Hamnett p.40 (right); Levis p.69 (right); Lulu Guiness p.9 (top); Paul Smith
p.14 (right); Paxar p.117; Rose Sinclair pp.79, 121, 130 (left and right); Science Photo Library p.114; Susi Paz pp.40 (left),
76(right); Transprints Ltd p.84 (all); V&A p.94 (left); Vilene p.75 Yiogos Nikiteas pp.34 (right), 100, 105.

Cover photograph by SPL
Cover design by Wooden Ark

Picture research by Susi Paz and Toria Townsley

The publisher would like to thank the following for permission to reproduce copyright material:

The Woolmark ® certification trade mark on page 46 is reproduced with permission of The Woolmark Company. The
commercial pattern on page 122 is reproduced courtesy of the McCall Pattern Company. The BEAB kitemark on p.52 is
reproduced with permission of ASTA BEAB Certification Services.

A special thanks to the students who allowed their coursework to be reproduced in this publication.

The publishers have made every effort to trace copyright holders. However, if any material has been incorrectly acknowledged,
we would be pleased to correct this at the earliest opportunity.

Contents

Introduction

This book has been written to meet the requirements of the full and short course AQA specifications for GCSE Textiles Technology. The AQA specification is designed to meet the National Curriculum Orders and GCSE Subject Criteria for Design and Technology.

The programme of study for Design and Technology at Key Stage 4 requires you to develop your Design and Technology capability by applying knowledge and understanding of textiles technology when developing ideas, planning, making products and evaluating them.

AQA specification

The specification provides opportunities for you to develop Design and Technology capability throughout your course. It requires you to combine skills with knowledge and understanding in order to design and make quality products in quantity. It also provides opportunities for you to acquire and apply knowledge, skills and understanding through:
* analysing and evaluating existing products and industrial processes
* undertaking focused practical tasks to develop and demonstrate techniques
* working out how to develop ideas, and plan and produce products
* considering how past and present design and technology affects society
* recognizing the moral, cultural and environmental issues in design and technology situations
* using ICT.

How will you be assessed?

You will be assessed in two ways. You will complete a coursework project making up 60 per cent of your GCSE mark. You will also complete a two hour (one hour for the short course) written exam at the end of the course that will make up 40 per cent of your GCSE mark. In both the coursework and the written exam, you will be assessed on how you demonstrate your knowledge, skills and understanding in three ways:
1 of materials, components, processes, techniques and industrial practice (20 per cent)
2 when designing and making quality products in quantity (60 per cent)
3 when evaluating processes and products and examining the wider effects of design and technology on society (20 per cent).

Most of your marks (60 per cent) will be awarded for designing and making. Most of your designing and making will be completed in your coursework project.

How to use this book

This book will help you:
* develop your textiles technology skills
* develop your knowledge and understanding of textiles technology, specifically for the content requirements of the AQA specification
* understand what is required for internal assessment (coursework) and how to get the best grades
* prepare and revise for the written exam and understand how to get the best grades
* develop key skills of communication, application of number, information and communication technology, working with others, problem solving and improving your own learning through your textiles technology work.

This book is divided into the following parts:
* Part 1 What you need to know: this is the main part of the book and contains Sections 1–7
* Part 2 Doing your coursework project: this contains Section 8 and gives advice on how to plan and produce your coursework, helping you get the best marks possible
* Part 3 Preparing for the exam: this comprises Section 9 and gives advice on what examiners are looking for, how to prepare for the exam and how to get the best marks you can.

This book is written in double-page chapters. Each chapter includes:
* specification links to show which modules of the AQA specification are covered by the chapter
* an introduction showing what you will learn from the chapter
* activities that reinforce and develop learning
* a summary of the chapter to help with revision.

Chapters that include an activity involving the use of ICT are identified by the ICT icon **ICT** at the top of the page.

AQA Textiles 10.5,10.6
Numbering is used on each double-paged chapter to show which section of the AQA Textiles specification the chapter matches.

c D1 Some chapters of Part 1 are also useful for the coursework project. This is identified by showing the relevant coursework assessment criteria at the top of the chapter. Here,

'D' refers to Designing and 'M' refers to Making. Along with the numbering, these are taken from the coursework project assessment criteria given in section 16.3 of the AQA specification. Please note that grades F and G have fewer assessment criteria, so the numbering here is based on grades A–E for consistency.

Some chapters might also include:

★ coursework boxes: these show how particular chapters in Part 1 are relevant to your coursework, so you should keep this information in mind when completing your project. You will also need to make sure you read Part 2 so that you understand exactly what you need to do for your project

★ case studies: these give real examples of how the processes and knowledge you are learning are applied in real life.

At the end of each section there are relevant examples of exam questions and the marks available. These will help you practise and revise for the exam.

Finally, there is also a glossary at the end of the book to explain words identified in bold text. This will be useful as you are going through your course and also when you come to revise for the exam or do your coursework.

Websites

There are links to relevant websites in this book. In order to ensure that the links are up-to-date, that the links work, and that the sites are not inadvertently linked to sites that could be considered offensive, we have made the links available on the Heinemann website at www.heinemann.co.uk/hotlinks. When you access the site, the express code is 349XP.

Short course

If you are following the short course, you will need to use just some of the chapters in this book. You will need guidance from your teacher on how to use this book and which chapters to use.

Design principles

This section concentrates on how to begin designing and the ways in which you can use design principles (the understanding of design) in your design projects. This will help you develop the skills necessary to design for different areas of the textiles industry, such as fashion, fabrics, interiors and accessories.

What's in this section?

Design, line and form

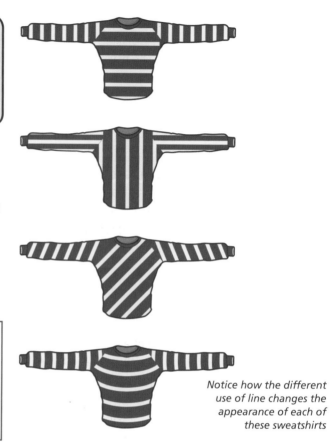

In this chapter you will:

★ learn what design is

★ learn the key principles of design and how to apply these to your own designs.

Design pervades all aspects of life; good design is essential in a product if it is to attract the consumer and be successful. Good design is pleasing to the client and meets all the functional requirements; that is, it meets the **design specification**.

The key principles of design are **line**, **pattern**, **form**, colour and **texture**. These are the tools you will use when designing.

Coursework

Line, form, colour, pattern and texture are the key principles or ideas that you need to follow when designing products. You will need to think about these both when designing your own products and when evaluating existing products.

Notice how the different use of line changes the appearance of each of these sweatshirts

Line

When applied to textiles, 'line' can refer to the fabric design (for example, a striped or checked pattern), or it may refer to the shape of the garment (for example, an A-line skirt or a raglan sleeve).

Lines are an important design tool because they can affect how we see and feel about products or, in the case of interior design, about rooms and spaces.

- Horizontal lines make a shape look and feel wider and shorter.
- Vertical lines add height and make a shape seem narrower.
- Diagonal lines can add a feeling of movement and, depending on which way they slant, can have the same effect as either vertical or horizontal lines.
- Curved lines emphasize curves on the body or on furniture and soften shapes.

Pattern

A pattern is a design which is made up of a combination of lines and shapes. It is repeated over the area of a fabric. Patterns can be complex or simple. When choosing a suitable pattern for a fabric, it is important to consider the purpose intended for the fabric. Sometimes a pattern can look quite different when the fabric has been cut and shaped; for example, a very large pattern would lose impact if cut into small pieces for a petite garment. Equally, a child-friendly, bright and colourful fabric would be out of place on business clothing.

Some patterns repeat over and over again; these are called repeat patterns. Care must be taken when cutting these so that the patterns match up. Checks and tartans are repeat patterns and it is very obvious if these are not matched. Regular patterns repeat but may not need matching; they may be too large or too small for a match to matter. Irregular patterns do not repeat evenly and do not need matching.

Patterns occur everywhere in our environment; both in the natural world, for example in flowers and rock formations, and in the man-made world, for example in buildings and street grids.

Colour

All designers use colour. It is important to think about the use of a product before deciding on its colour. Colours can affect the mood and style of the design or the product user. For example blue and green are regarded as cool colours, whereas red, orange and yellow are hot colours. Colours can also be combined together in pattern. You will learn more about colour in Chapter 1.2.

Form

Form refers to the 2D or 3D shape of a product. Shape may be described as **organic** (natural) such as shells, or **inorganic** (man-made) such as geometric shapes including circles, squares and buildings. Shape can be used to give an unusual illusion to a product. For example, the designer Lulu Guinness designed a bag in the shape of a pair of lips.

A Lulu Guinness bag in the form of a pair of lips

Texture

Texture describes what the surface of a product feels and looks like. In textiles and fashion products, the feel of a fabric is important as people like to wear products that feel good against the skin. Texture can also increase the properties of the product. For example, a fur fabric used for a winter hat will trap a layer of air round the wearer's head and make it warmer. It is very important to choose the right fabric for the intended purpose. The high sheen created by satin fabric is suitable for evening wear as it reflects light and gives a very elegant, sensual look to the garment. However, this would not be appropriate for a uniform where a more formal and serviceable image is needed.

Texture or surface decoration can also be added to fabrics using techniques such as embroidery and printing.

Activities

1 Create four designs for a pair of smart trousers for either a man or a woman using the design principles.

2 Evaluate each design to show how appropriate it is for the client.

3 Choose a natural object such as a shell or a leaf. How many different pattern designs can you create that use lines based solely on this natural shape?

Summary

★ All the elements add visual effects, which make you like or dislike a product.

★ When designing a product, you must make sure that you consider its use and function. You must create products that meet the specification and that are attractive to the client.

★ Line, pattern, colour, form and texture will all help you to develop your design to meet the needs of the specification and inform your client.

Design principles

Colour in textiles and fashion

1.2

In this chapter you will:

★ learn what colour is and how it is chosen

★ learn why colour is important in design

★ learn that colour is also related to ethnicity and culture.

What is colour?

Colour is created by the reflection and absorption of light by a surface. Colour is one of the most important elements in the design of a product. It plays a major role in textiles and fashion products, and it is one of the first things people notice. People use colour to determine whether or not they like a product and their feelings towards it.

Designing with colour

When designing products, different colours are used to convey different meanings or to make the user feel a certain way. Colour affects people both emotionally and physically. Pastel colours, such as pink, are considered calming, whereas orange is considered young and energetic, and red may signal danger. Reds and yellows are described as warm colours, whereas blues and greys are described as cold colours. Dark colours, such as charcoal grey or navy blue, are often chosen to give an efficient and businesslike feel to a uniform or business suit.

The use of certain colours in interior decorating can make rooms look very different. Dark colours can make a room seem smaller and more closed in. Light colours can make the room appear larger and more open.

It should also be remembered that colour choices are very personal and a client may choose a particular colour or colour scheme for no reason other than that they particularly like it.

Coursework

Remember that when designing a product you must consider who it is for and what the use will be, and then use the principles of design to help you meet the specification.

Colour forecasting

In the fashion and textiles industry, colour is an important factor; it is used to determine key trends in design. Specialized companies, called prediction and trend forecasting companies, develop books or websites devoted to predicting what colours will be used on what products. Each part of the industry will choose particular colours depending on the market that their product is aimed at.

Colours and culture

Cultural differences also need to be considered when using colour in design because different cultures attach distinct meanings to colour. For example, in Hindu culture, the colour red is symbolic of purity, but in the West it represents danger or sexual passion. Designers have to be very careful how they use red on products to be sold to the Hindu market. The table below shows some of the ways different cultures and nations view colours.

Colour		Cultural association
Black		West: mourning/death; elegance
White		East: mourning/death West: purity and weddings
Red		China: celebration and luck – used at both funerals and weddings Hinduism: purity and weddings West: danger, ceremonial
Blue		China: immortality Judaism: holiness Hinduism: colour of the God Krishna
Green		Islam: sacred colour Some tropical countries: associations with danger West: safe colour, nature and the environment Ireland: religious significance (Catholic)
Yellow		Hinduism: sacred colour West: Easter, spring
Orange		West: Halloween Ireland: religious significance (Protestant)

Cultural associations with colour

The colour wheel

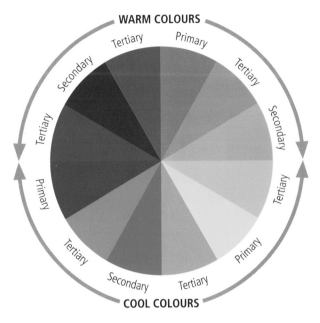

The colour wheel

The colour wheel is used by designers to split colours into different colour groups. The groups are:
- primary colours – red, yellow and blue – are the colours from which all others are created
- secondary colours occur where two primary colours are combined, such as green (yellow and blue), orange (yellow and red) and purple (red and blue)
- tertiary colours are made by mixing one primary and one secondary colour.

Colours can then be divided into two main categories.
- Complementary – use of different colours, such as orange and blue, can create a balancing effect. Complementary colours tend to be opposite each other on the colour wheel.
- Harmonious – colours with similar hues give a varied but subtle, harmonious effect. These are next to each other on the colour wheel.

Colours can also be put into groups according to:
- hue – the actual colour that you see
- shade – a variety of colour when black is added
- tone – a variety of colour when white is added.

One final way of grouping colours is to divide them into **monochromatic** and **achromatic** colours. Monochromatic colours contain the shades, tints and hues of one colour. Achromatic colours have no colour, so they only use black, grey or white.

Applying colour to products

Colour is applied to textiles products either by printing or by dyeing. You will learn more about this later in Chapters 5.10 and 5.11. Colour can also be added through embroidery.

? Test your knowledge

1 What are complementary colours?

2 Explain why culture plays an important part in the colours that designers choose for products.

 Activities

1 Create a simple design for a cushion and show how the design could change with the use of:
- contrasting colours
- complementary colours
- tones or tints.

2 Explain how each of these could affect the mood or feel of a room.

Summary

★ Designers use colour to make their products appeal to different people; they try to predict which colours will sell best.

★ Colours can look hot, cold, heavy, light, dark, near or far, and can influence emotions.

★ Colours have different meanings depending on the culture that you come from.

Design principles

Designing for fashion

In this chapter you will:

★ learn that designing for the fashion market is very complex as it is divided into different segments

★ learn that designing for fashion requires you to look at both past and future trends, as well as at the different fabrics that are available

★ learn that designs will be different depending on the market the product is aimed at.

What is fashion?

Fashion is a style of clothing that is popular at a particular point in time. There are many reasons behind the fashion choices people make and, in order to be successful as a designer, you must consider them all. Your designs will need to be different depending on the market they are aimed at. Clothes serve many functions.

- Protection: clothes are called utility products as they are used for a range of needs. For example, we need clothes to protect us from hot or cold weather, such as sun hats or coats, or to protect us from harm or injury, such as protective gloves.

- Modesty: modern society's conventions dictate that we use clothes to cover our bodies.

- Adornment: clothes help us to look good. However, certain fashions do not always make us comfortable. For example, corsets were very fashionable in the 1800s but they distorted women's bodies and were painful to wear.

- Symbolism: clothing may indicate someone's status, such as a judge, vicar or religious leader.

- Social style: clothing may identify people as part of a particular group. The dandies of the 1800s, the mods and rockers of the 1960s or the 'urban' cultures of today all have their own styles.

- Psychological: clothes can be used to help someone assert their own personality, such as power dressing business suits.

- Modernism: the part of the world people come from can affect the clothes that they wear, as can the ethnic culture they are a part of.

- Ethical: some people are concerned about how their clothes are produced; there is a growing trend to wear clothes that are recycled or are made from sustainable resources, such as cotton or linen, that can be replanted and cause no damage to the environment.

- Technological: increasingly, people want clothes that interact with their bodies and with their electronic gadgets. Designers are responding to this by creating 'smart' clothing which responds to the wearer's needs.

Clothing often identifies people within a particular social group, as is the case with the distinctive fashion of these 1960s 'mods'

Influences from the past

Designers get inspiration from a wide range of sources including street fashion, haute couture and designs of the past. Fashion is often described as a cycle, which means that the fashions we see today often appeared years ago in a slightly different form. In the 1940s, for example, the 'new' fashion for women was called the 'wasp waist'. The idea was that the waist should look tiny, and this was emphasized through corsets and full skirts. This was not a new idea, however, but was borrowed from the corsets and large skirts of the Victorian era. The designer Vivienne Westwood used the same idea again in the 1990s. We can see this trend in the pictures opposite. Designers will re-do or re-work past styles to make them more contemporary.

The cycle of fashion: corsets popular in the 1950s and again in 2004

Other garments have changed a great deal in style or purpose over the years because of changing cultural demands. For example, the T-shirt was originally part of the uniform of French soldiers in the First World War. It was then adopted by American soldiers and used as uniform underwear during the Second World War. When the actor Marlon Brando wore a T-shirt as an outer garment in the film *A Streetcar Named Desire*, in 1951, it caused great scandal as he was considered to be wearing underwear in public. Since then the T-shirt has become a fashion garment worn by people from different cultures, genders, ages and social profiles.

New materials

Fashion is also influenced by materials. New fabrics are developed for particular purposes, but the fashion industry then uses them for other applications. For example, the original GorTex® garments were designed for extreme sportswear conditions as GorTex® is a waterproof and breathable fabric. Now, however, it is used on everyday garments such as jackets and coats. It is an expensive fabric but people are prepared to pay for fashionable looks.

The fashion industry

The fashion industry is divided into different areas because people have many different requirements from clothing. The specialist areas may be defined by age (for example, children's clothes) and gender (for example, women's clothes) as well

as by product or garment type (for example, sportswear and formal wear). Different types of garment tend to be made by different manufacturers. Each manufacturer develops its own particular expertise in the production and designing of those garments. Women's wear is the most rapidly changing area within fashion design, whereas the men's wear and children's wear fashion markets change more slowly.

The industry is further split into:
- haute couture, a French phrase meaning 'high tailoring', is the sector of the market that produces exclusive unique designs, which are often featured in the catwalk fashion shows. This is the most expensive end of the market
- prêt-à-porter is the ready-to-wear range. It is often designed by top designers but the garments are produced in bulk to be sold through high-class shops rather than through fashion houses
- high street retailers are the shops found in every high street with a mass-produced range of less expensive clothes. These are often based on the haute couture and ready-to-wear collections of top designers.

【Ic】 Coursework

When designing textiles products, you need to consider who the product is aimed at and endeavour to meet the needs of that market.

✎ Activities

1 Using the Internet, and any other appropriate sources, investigate how Vivienne Westwood used corsets in her designs and adapted them to modern life. Think about her use of the design principles.

2 Consider some of the ways this affected the fashion industry at the time.

Summary

★ Designers use a wide range of tools and fabrics to design for fashion.

★ Designers also design for specific areas of the market and must consider the needs of their particular market in order to make sure their designs meet those needs.

Design principles

In this chapter you will:

★ learn about the textile design industry

★ learn about creating textile designs for interior products.

The textile design market is split into three main sectors:

- clothing and accessories
- domestic products including sheets, towels, shower curtains, decorative pillows, tablecloths and napkins
- upholstery including drapery (curtains), wall coverings, and furniture.

Textile design is mainly concerned with **aesthetics**, the beauty of a fabric, and **handle**, how the fabric feels. Famous furnishing textiles designers include William Morris, companies such as Liberty and more recently Cath Kidston.

Cath Kidston is a popular modern textiles designer

Textile design can be separated into three areas:

- constructed textiles, which includes woven or knitted fabrics
- surface pattern textiles, which includes dyeing, printing and resist dyeing fabrics (for example, **batik**)
- surface decoration or embellishment of fabrics, for example embroidery and **appliqué**.

Designing textiles for interiors is an extensive area of expertise, and designers will usually just concentrate on one market. Some designers will adapt their designs for different markets such as the fashion designer Paul Smith who uses his famous striped textile designs for different products.

A design by Paul Smith

A wide range of fabrics is used for interior products. The interiors industry also uses colour, trends and innovation in the design of the products, just as in the clothing and fashion products industry.

Designing textiles for interior products

When designing fabrics for interior products, the following design considerations need to be met.

- Product: what is the product? Will it be mass-produced or one-off? Which room or interior is it for? How many colours should it have?
- Client: who is the client? What likes and dislikes does the client have? What age is the client?
- Fabric construction: will the fabric be printed, knitted or woven?
- Suitability of the fabric: is it right for its purpose? For example, if curtains are intended to cut down draughts and to insulate a room, they need to be made from a closely woven thick fabric such as velvet.
- How much use will the product get? This is an important consideration as it enables the designer to choose the appropriate material and fabric construction.

- Where will the product go? For example, if the room is large, then it may be possible to have bolder, more colourful designs than in a small room where something too large, bright or bold may be overpowering.
- Safety standards. The fabric needs to conform to high safety standards, especially those relating to flammability.
- Design considerations also need to look at the following: fabric, filling, joints and seams, and labelling.

As with clothing design, it is important for the interior textile designer to consider the design principles of line, form and colour in order to meet the needs of the user. The designer must always think about *who* it is for, *how* they will use it and *where* it is to be situated.

Types of pattern designs

There are a number of different types of patterns in textile design:

- motifs and styles: these can be realistic or stylized designs such as florals
- conversationals: designs based on pictures of actual objects
- geometrics: designs based on geometric shapes such as squares and circles
- contemporary: designs based on highly stylized motifs and simple geometric shapes, as well as typefaces and calligraphy (script)
- ethnic: designs with a strong cultural heritage such as African batik and Scottish Fair Isle
- chintz: a floral pattern, usually reserved for home furnishings, with bold, strong, contrasting colours.

The pattern is put into repeat in order to create a decorative surface. It is important that the designs are 'balanced' and laid out well. To do this, designers need to take into consideration three things: colour, layout and scale.

Computer aided design of fabrics

Many textile companies now use computer aided design (**CAD**) for the design and development of their products. With CAD they are able to re-colour designs quickly, resize patterns, create 'virtual designs' and create fabrics samples using digital printing techniques.

They can also re-colour designs to match the client's corporate colours or designs and repeat in different ways.

Once designs are created, they are transferred onto fabrics using a range of methods, for example screen-printing or digital printing. You will learn more about these methods in Chapters 5.10 and 5.11.

Safety testing

Fabrics for interior products need to undergo strict safety tests for **flammability** and **toxicity**, and they must follow the key legislation and BSI (British Standards Institute) requirements. This is because of the toxic fumes these products can give off when they burn, which has led to many deaths. New flame retardant finishes and foams (used in chairs and cushions) are now being used. The designer needs to consider these requirements when designing for interiors. You will learn more about testing and the safety of fabrics in Chapters 4 and 7.

🖪 **Coursework**

You need to make clear who your product is intended for, where it is to go, and what other items it may have to complement.

✏ **Activities**

1 Design a pair of curtains for a small bedroom which is situated in the attic and has sloping walls.

2 Explain how these would need to be changed to suit a large, first floor bedroom with patio style doors opening onto a balcony.

Summary

★ The same principles of design apply to both furnishing textiles and fashion design, with the needs of the client being the most important.

★ CAD is a useful tool when designing fabrics for interior products.

Design principles

Exam questions

1 You are the designer for a manufacturing company. A client has asked you to use inspiration from the shape, pattern, colours and texture of insects to design and make an original and exciting product that will sell well.

Give two different ways of finding out about insects

(2 marks)

2 You can use the colours, shapes and patterns linked with insects to give you ideas.

a How could you use colour? *(3 marks)*

b How could you use shape? *(3 marks)*

c How could you use pattern? *(3 marks)*

(AQA 2003)

2 Project skills

This section covers the range of different skills that you will need in order to develop your coursework portfolio, and when designing and making textiles products. This includes research, designing and developing ideas.

What's in this section?

Project skills

Design briefs and task analysis

In this chapter you will:
★ learn what a design brief is and how it is used
★ learn how to develop a design brief.

What is a design brief?

A **design brief** is a key document that is drawn up by the client to guide the designer in the design process. A design brief can have a specific theme or be open ended for the designer to interpret. You will use a design brief as the starting point for your coursework; you will be able to explore the possibilities in the design brief and use it to demonstrate your skills in designing and making. The examination also follows the design process and you will need to be able to explain how to use and develop the design brief. For example:

- in an 'open' brief, there is no specific theme and it is left to the designer to develop the design theme. No final design solution or product is specified, for example, 'Design a range of Halloween products'.

- in a 'closed' brief, the design brief has specific guidelines in terms of product, colour and theme, and target market. Here, the final design solution is specified, for example, 'Design a range of Halloween costumes for 11–16 year olds'.

Components of the design brief

The key things that will be highlighted by the client in the design brief are:

- *a market overview of their current products: who buys their product, where do they sell the most products*
- *who their main competitors are*
- what products they want the designer to design
- *the completion date for the project*
- key colours to include or avoid; logos or company (corporate) colours
- whether it is a new product or the redesigning of an existing product
- the price range of the products to be designed
- the scale of manufacturing: where the product will be manufactured and in what quantities, as this will have an effect on the overall cost of the product.

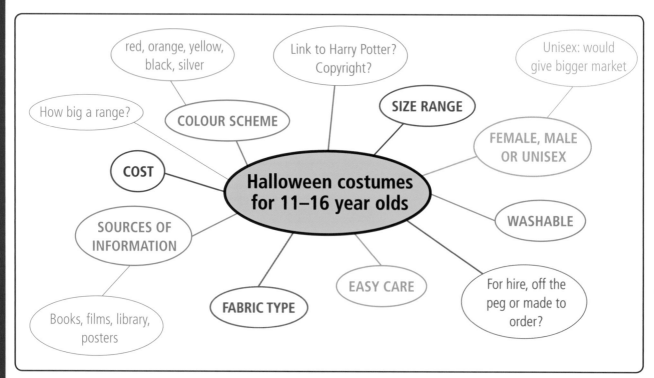

Analysing the design brief

The design brief forms a discussion document between you as designer and the client so that you can arrive at a suitable solution. When working from your own design brief in your coursework, you may be working for an imaginary client and may not need to consider the factors shown in italics in the list above. Your teacher may suggest some suitable design briefs for the class and then help you to begin the analysis of them. This will form the starting point for your work.

Task analysis

Once you have your design brief you must understand what you are being asked to do and how this could be achieved. It is a good idea to draw an ideas map showing what you already know and what you need to find out. You could also include details of where you might find the information. Ask yourself *what* do I need to find out and *where* will I find the information? This will form the plan for your research.

When you know what you are being asked to do, you need to carry out some research to find out how you should do it.

The ideas map above shows what an analysis of the design brief 'Design a range of Halloween costumes for 11–16 year olds' could look like.

Coursework

Task analysis is an important part of the analysis section of your design folder, and without this you will limit your marks for analysis.

Test your knowledge

1 How does a clear analysis of the design brief help the designer?

Summary

★ The design brief is used by the client to give the designer a clear guide to the product to be designed and should present a focus for their inspiration.

★ The task analysis is used to guide the designer on what they need to research before they can start designing. This needs to be carried out very carefully in order to make sure that the final product meets the design brief.

Activities

Using the following design brief, draw an ideas map that analyses the brief and gives the designer a clear idea of the requirements of the client and where to find the relevant information. Use the example opposite to help you.

'Design a range of cartoon character fancy dress costumes for 7–10 year olds to be sold through a popular supermarket chain.'

As well as the points mentioned earlier, you may need to think about:

- the type of customer the supermarket attracts
- the price range
- how much space is available on the shop floor
- the 'pester power' of children shopping with their parents.

Project skills

Research skills

In this chapter you will:
★ learn what types of research there are
★ find out where you get information from
★ learn how you use it.

What is research?

Research will form the starting point for all of your work. Research is:

- finding information that can help you to design your product
- analysing this information
- drawing conclusions from it that will enable you to move on with your own designs.

The theme for your research will come from your analysis of your design brief. This will help you to focus on the best way to meet the design brief. You need to include information about customer preferences, costing, fabric types and possible decorative techniques, as well as any specific points raised in your task analysis. The information collected from your research needs to be retained so that you can refer to it. However, when doing your coursework project, you will only present the results of your research in your folder.

The information that you collect will consist of both written and visual information and will come from a range of sources. These can be either **primary sources** or **secondary sources**.

Primary sources

Primary sources are those where information does not necessarily already exist. Information is gathered at first hand, so primary sources might include:

- questionnaires
- surveys
- exhibitions
- photographs
- sketches
- shop visits
- product analysis: product analysis is a really important aspect of understanding how a product is manufactured

and knowing about the materials it is made from. You will learn more about product analysis in Chapter 2.4.

Look at this design brief: 'Design a range of bags to be used for carrying sports clothing and equipment.' Primary research for this design brief could include:

- a visit to a sports shop to see what is already available: the styles, cost, colour range and fabrics of existing products. You may also be able to find out which designs are the best sellers
- talking to sports players to find out what they need to carry
- sketching some ideas and showing them to possible users so that you can collect their comments
- carrying out a product analysis on an existing product
- designing a questionnaire and asking a range of people for their ideas about the product.

Questionnaires

A questionnaire is a useful tool with which to gather information. It will allow you to present the results in graph or chart form, which will help your **ICT** marks. You could even email it to potential users. You will learn more about questionnaires in Chapter 2.3.

Secondary sources

Secondary sources are those where information about a particular subject has already been collected. Secondary sources include books, magazines, museums, the Internet and CD-ROMs.

Statistics are also used as a way of obtaining information. For instance, shops use statistics to see how many products have been sold or which products are most popular.

Secondary research for the design brief 'Design a range of bags to be used for carrying sports clothing and equipment' could include:

- looking in magazines for illustrations (if you use these in your project, you must annotate them)
- using the Internet to access a manufacturer's website to find information about existing products
- using software to access a **database** and find information about types of fabrics and their properties.

Design inspiration

As well as written research, you need to collate a range of visual resources. This is called **design inspiration** and will help you develop ideas for your product. Design inspiration includes colour, texture, shape and pattern. Designers in industry display information in sketchbooks or on layout boards to help focus their ideas on the theme of their work. Design inspiration can come from a range of sources, such as:

- nature: plants, the sea and sea life, animals, birds, landscapes
- architecture: the shape, style and colour of buildings
- texture: fabric swatches
- travel: interesting pictures of the places visited when travelling around the world
- geometric patterns: circles and squares or more complex shapes such as pentagons and hexagons
- artistic influences: for example, Impressionist painters or Pop Art such as that by Andy Warhol
- photographs, film and the cinema: a film might inspire you to find out more information about a country, or might inspire the type of clothes that can be developed. A photograph might give you an idea for a pattern or theme.

Ic Coursework

As part of your coursework portfolio, you will need to show how you have collected a range of research information that is relevant to your chosen design brief. The research section of your coursework should be brief and should only take up two or three pages of A3 paper.

? Test your knowledge

1 Give two examples of primary research and two examples of secondary research.

2 What is design inspiration and how might it be used in your work?

Summary

★ Good research is an essential part of the development process of a project.

★ It is important to collect information from both primary and secondary sources.

This moodboard shows design inspiration taken from the theme of leaves

Project skills

How to write a questionnaire

In this chapter you will:
★ learn how to write a questionnaire
★ learn how to use the results of your questionnaire.

Questionnaires are a very good way of gathering primary research from a range of people. To be effective they must be carefully planned so that you obtain the type of information that you need.

First, you need to think carefully about exactly what you want to find out so that you can structure your questions accordingly. Next, you need to know who the product is aimed at so that your sample group includes people who are likely to use the product. Sometimes the user and the buyer may not be the same as when, for example, you are designing for children. If this is the case, you may need two different questionnaires or different sections in one questionnaire for each group to answer. A good questionnaire will give you information about your target group's preferences; their likes and dislikes.

How to write a questionnaire

There are two types of question that may be used in a questionnaire: **open questions** and **closed questions**. Open questions allow people to write in whatever answer they choose. Closed questions ask people to select an answer from a range of given answers. Although open questions allow people to give more detailed answers, it can be difficult to analyse the results as the answers may be very long and you may not be able to count the responses easily. If you supply a range of answers and tick boxes, it becomes much easier to collate and analyse the results. Look at the example in the box below.

Question 1	Which style of jeans do you prefer?
Question 2	Which style of jeans do you prefer?
	a. Bootleg
	b. Straight
	c. Loose fit
	d. Stretch

Question 1 is an open question and question 2 is a closed question. Question 1 could yield many different or lengthy answers that do not give the information needed. The author of question 2 wants to know about four specific styles of jeans, and this question will give them the answers they need. Sometimes it is helpful to include a range within the answer options, as in question 2, which makes it easier to control the answers given.

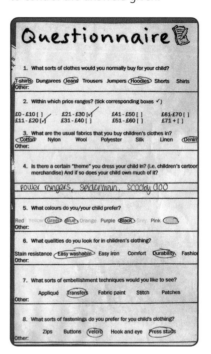

A student's questionnaire

Analysing the results

When you have constructed your questionnaire and asked your sample group to complete it, you need to analyse the results. The easiest and clearest way to do this is to use a spreadsheet programme to display your results as graphs or charts using chart wizard. This enables you to present your results very clearly in a visual way. It will also help you display your ICT skills.

When you have produced your graphs and charts, you need to include a summary explaining what you have learned from the questionnaire. This will help you to write your design specification.

Analysing the information collected from a questionnaire will help you draw conclusions about your design work. Use the following questions to analyse your results.

Style of jeans	Number of people preferring that style
Bootleg	15
Straight	4
Loose fit	10
Stretch	6

Price of jeans	Number of people prepared to pay that price
£10-15	4
£15-20	5
£20-30	15
£30-40	10
£40+	6

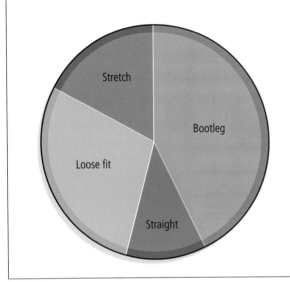

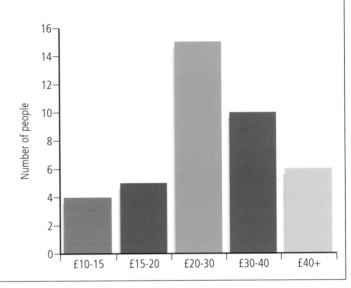

Pie charts and bar charts are helpful ways of showing your results

- What are the main things that the users prefer?
- How will the results affect your design specification?
- Do the questions help you to make decisions about the colour, shape, cost, size, weight and function of the product(s) you will make?

Questionnaires can also be used when evaluating your product or design ideas. You can ask users what they think of your product and can make improvements based on the information you gather.

Coursework

Questionnaires help you decide on design criteria. You should not include all the copies of your questionnaire in your folder, just the results, the graphs and charts together with a summary.

Activity

Write a questionnaire with five questions to gather information about a textiles product you want to design and make. Use closed questions to do this and remember that you need to find out about the needs of the target group, the place of sale, the cost and size of the product. Present your results in a range of graphs and charts.

Summary

★ A questionnaire is a very useful tool for gathering primary research.

★ Open questions should be used very carefully as they are difficult to analyse. It is much easier to analyse data from closed questions.

★ Questionnaires can also be used as part of the ongoing evaluation process.

Project skills

Product analysis and evaluation

In this chapter you will:

★ learn what product analysis is and why it is an important tool for the designer

★ discover key ways in which a product can be analysed.

Product analysis is part of the research you should carry out so that you can design and make quality products. To analyse a product means to examine it in detail. If you are thinking of making a certain product and want to find out more about it, you need to examine some existing products that are the same. Whether you are designing garments, accessories or fabrics, you will use product analysis as a way of understanding how the product or the fabric works. This in turn helps you to develop designs that enhance or use the features of the fabric or product. To do this you need to:

- disassemble the product (take it apart)
- look at the information on the care label or swing tag to find out about the fibres used in the product and their care
- analyse your own design ideas to help you decide on a final product specification.

What to look for

When analysing a product, you should look at the following.

- Whether it is suitable for the intended purpose or user.
- How the designer has used line, form and colour in their designs to make it appropriate for the user.
- The quality of the product.
- How it is joined together, for example its seams.
- The texture on the surface of the fabrics. Was it added during manufacture, for example calendaring, or was it added after manufacturing, for example stitching/ embroidering?
- How colour was applied. Was it printed? If so, which method was used? Was it dyed? If so, how or when in the production process was the dye applied?
- The number of stages needed to make the product or the possible types of equipment needed to make it.

Product analysis

When developing new products, designers will look at existing products. This is called product analysis and is primary research. When you analyse a product, you will learn from other designers' ideas, but you will also get to know that product well so that you do not copy it by mistake. Evaluating existing products is key to understanding what makes a product good or bad and judging whether it does its job well or not.

Looking at existing products also develops inspiration and creativity. Products can be modified to improve them or to make them suitable for more clients. One designer who does this is Vivienne Westwood, who takes apart old garments and uses the shapes she finds to help her design new ones. One example of this is her corset designs, which set a new fashion for corset-style bodices.

Disassembly

A good way to learn about an existing product is to disassemble it. This means to take it apart, unpick it and reduce it back to the flat pieces of fabric it was made from. This could be done as a group exercise and you could just take apart half of the garment in order to save time.

By disassembling a product, you are trying to discover the original shapes of the garment pieces, the interfacing used, the fabric used and the way in which it has been cut out. You will need to press the pieces flat with an iron in order to see the shapes clearly. You can then draw it to keep a record of what it looked like. You can also look at the label to see which fabrics the manufacturer has used to make the product.

Disassembly increases a designer's knowledge of manufacturing techniques. It also improves knowledge of the function of the product and its components so that they can be improved. The designer must be able to look at a product and assess how it can be used by a variety of users, or be adapted for a new range of users.

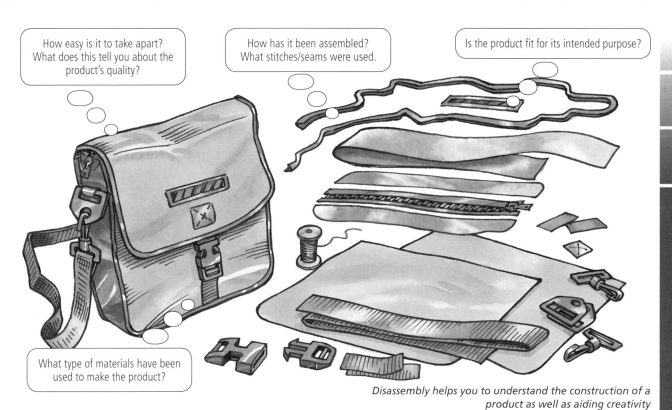

Disassembly helps you to understand the construction of a product as well as aiding creativity

Increasing knowledge about materials

Disassembly or product analysis also helps a designer to understand how the materials that they use for a product operate under different conditions. It also aids their understanding of the safety conditions that might need to be applied in the manufacture or use of the product. For example, if you disassemble a fur fabric product, you will see just how much loose fur is produced. This highlights the effect this could have on workers with asthma and stresses the need for very good ventilation in the manufacturing situation.

Test your knowledge

1 What does the term 'product analysis' mean?
2 How can you use product analysis?

Activities

In a group, take apart half of an old garment, unpick the seams, iron it flat and work out how much fabric would be needed to cut it out from a length of 150 cm wide plain fabric.

Coursework

★ You will need to analyse existing products when doing the research for your own product. Looking at what is available will help you to find a gap in the market for something new or slightly different.

★ You will also need to analyse your own design ideas to help you decide on a final design solution. In order to select and reject your ideas, you must give your reasons for doing so.

Summary

★ Product analysis can help designers understand the following:
  • how a product is used
  • what materials it is made of and how it was produced
  • how well it meets the needs of the end-user.

★ Product analysis gives designers a better understanding of other products on the market.

Project skills

Analysis of research

In this chapter you will:
★ learn how to analyse research
★ learn how to write a design specification.

Your research should have increased your understanding of your design brief and given you a starting point for your design specification. You now need to ask yourself what you have learned and how it will influence your **design specification**.

Analysis of research

Your research can include a mixture of visual and written information. While you are collecting information, you need to make sure that that you note down where you got the information from in case you need to refer to it again. It is important that you assess the information you have gathered to make sure that it is really relevant.

Once you have collected the information, you must now draw some conclusions. You need to decide how to use the information to make a quality product that fits the design brief. To do this, you will need to analyse your research in terms of the following factors.

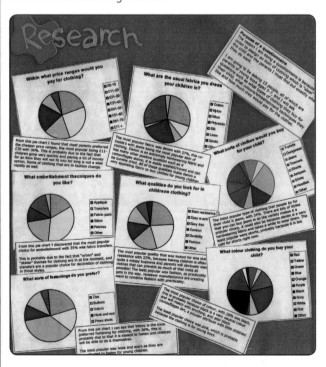

- How information you have collected relates to your design brief. How will this help you to meet the brief?
- Feedback received from the client or potential user of your product about what they like, and how it might relate to the product that they want. Other factors to consider may be, for example, the age of the client, their social background, gender or culture.
- The type of fabrics that might be best for the end product.
- Which colours will be relevant to your design.
- Environmental issues that may need to be considered. For example, is the product to be recycled or could it be made from recycled materials?
- whether the choice of fabrics or other processes will affect the cost of the product.

Presenting your research

After you have analysed your research, you need to present your findings. It is important that you only present the *results* of your research in your project. Ask yourself *what* you have learned from your research and *how* you are going to use it. To help you do this, consider the following questions.

- What is important about the information that you have found?
- How do you think you might be able to use the information in your project?
- Do you have enough of the right information? Will you need to get some more?

You also need to:

- think about ways of using the information in your portfolio
- highlight visual information that can be used as starting points for design ideas.

When you have completed your research and analysed it, you will be able to write your design specification, and begin to think about developing your ideas further.

It is important to analyse your research thoroughly and present your findings

A student's design specification along with some design ideas

[ic] **Coursework**

★ Remember that you need to keep the research and the analysis to between two and three sheets of A3 paper, but these should be packed with information.

★ It is important that you give some thought as to how you are going to present your results. Marks are awarded for the use of ICT, so if you present your results clearly in graph or chart form, or perhaps by using spreadsheets, you will add to your ICT marks. You will also ensure that your work will be clear.

Your design specification should include details of the product including:

• the size
• the function
• the materials and their properties
• the shape
• the cost
• the theme
• any environmental issues such as whether the materials will be recycled later, and the environmental costs of fabric care and materials used
• the techniques that will be used to make it.

Design specification

The design specification, or design criteria, is a series of requirements that set the restrictions within which you are going to work. It should also be divided into **essential criteria** – elements that the design specification must have; and **desirable criteria** – elements that you would like the design specification to have. For example, 'it is *essential* that the cushion measures 50 cm × 50 cm and it would be *desirable* for it to be washable'.

✏ **Activity**

Write a design specification for a sports bag for a teenage basketball player of either sex. Include four essential criteria and two desirable criteria.

Summary

★ The design specification provides the framework into which the design ideas must fit.

Project skills

Developing and filtering ideas

In this chapter you will:
★ learn how to sort out your ideas and select the most appropriate one.

Design ideas

When you have written your design specification, you need to look at the essential and desirable criteria and start to produce ideas that will match them. You should produce a range of designs that meet the criteria, sketch them and fully annotate them to describe the features you have included. It is essential that the ideas can be fully understood by your client, so you need to include styling details, colourways and fabric information with your ideas.

Evaluation

Evaluation helps you to decide what to do next and is a very important part of the designing and making procedure. All the way through the design and making processes, you need to analyse and evaluate the success of your work and record this by putting your thoughts down on paper. **Formative evaluation** takes place at each stage of your work and **summative evaluation** takes place at the end of all your work.

You need to use formative evaluation to help you filter your ideas, as you may find that not all of your ideas match all of the specification points. It may help you to filter your ideas if you produce a table like the one opposite to remind you of the criteria you are trying to match.

Looking at the table, ideas 5, 6 and 7 match all the criteria given and so would be a more suitable match than ideas 1, 2, 3 and 4, which all lack one criteria. You may choose to alter ideas 1–4 or discard them and choose one of the others as your final design. You will not have time to try out all your ideas, so take the time to think about the merits of each design and choose carefully.

Developing your ideas

Using the results of your evaluation, you can develop or modify your design where necessary. You need to show how you have modified or developed your design idea to improve it. There are many ways that you can do this.
- By changing the colour of all or part of your design.
- By changing the size; this could also include altering a commercial pattern to make it fit.
- By enhancing the product with decoration.
- By adding extra details such as pockets, top stitching or pleats.
- By testing the possibility of using different types of fabric.
- By changing the fastenings.

All of these would change and develop your design; you must remember that any development must meet the design specification. All modifications should improve the performance or quality of the end product. When you have completed your modifications to your final design, you will be ready to write your product specification.

Your design ideas should include sketches and full annotation

Specification criteria	Idea 1	Idea 2	Idea 3	Idea 4	Idea 5	Idea 6	Idea 7
Cost no more than £5	✓	✓	✗	✗	✓	✓	✓
Be washable	✓	✓	✓	✓	✓	✓	✓
Have a decorated pocket	✗	✓	✓	✓	✓	✓	✓
Be colourfast	✓	✗	✓	✓	✓	✓	✓
Suitable for children aged 7–10 years	✓	✓	✓	✓	✓	✓	✓
Sold through mail order	✓	✓	✓	✓	✓	✓	✓

Do the design ideas match the specification criteria?

Writing a product specification

When you have decided on your final product, you need to write a **product specification**. The product specification is a much more detailed description of the final product than the design specification. The product specification describes a particular product and is used by manufacturing companies to help make, as well as sell, their products. If you look at these two examples, you can see how a product specification differs from a design specification.

Design specification for a child's dress:
- It must be suitable for a young child.
- It must come in a range of sizes.
- It must be hard wearing.
- It must be washable.
- It may be sleeveless.
- It would be preferable if it were decorated.

Product specification for a child's dress:
- Age — dress suitable for a young child aged 4–8 years
- Size range — 4–8 years, sized according to British Standard sizing
- Fabric — denim (hard wearing fabric)
- Fibre — cotton
- Colour — dark blue (see sample), colourfast
- Fabric weight — medium (see sample)
- Care — washable (using colourfast dye)
- Style — A-line; no seam in the front; centre back seam with 15 cm cotton zipper at the neck; one 10 cm square pocket on the right-hand side of the skirt front, 4 cm below the waist line; no sleeves; neck and armhole finished with a contrast bias facing; 3 cm hem sewn with blind machine stitch.

Coursework

★ You must show a range of suitable initial design ideas and not just the same one with minor changes.

★ You must show how and why you have modified your product. You need to justify your modifications as in, for example, 'I have changed the buttons on the child's jacket to toggles, which are larger and easier for the child to manage. I have also changed the fabric from silk to cotton as it is easier to wash.'

Summary

★ Your design ideas should come as a result of the criteria included in your design specification.

★ You need to filter your design ideas to just one idea that can then be modified to improve it.

Activity

Look at the design ideas shown on this page, evaluate them and show how one of them could be modified.

Project skills

Design skills: sketching

In this chapter you will:

★ **learn about communicating your ideas**

★ **develop sketching skills**

★ **learn about tools that can be used for sketching.**

Sketching

Sketching ideas is a useful part of the design process as it allows you to develop your thinking and will help you see how your ideas will look. It is a good way to communicate your ideas to other people.

Good **annotation** around your sketches will inform the client or examiner about the details of your designs. Annotation means adding notes, which will explain what you are thinking or identify ways of developing your ideas further. Sketches allow you to record your ideas and will help you show the way that you have developed the designs that you made following your research.

Sketching allows you to be creative and experiment with different **techniques**, without the expense of making them. You could try to use several different sketching

techniques in your drawings, such as:

- using different types of pen or pencil to draw with
- using different colours
- using rubbings or illustrations of different surfaces to show texture in the fabric
- using small pieces of fabric pinned or glued onto the sketches; this will allow you to show how fabric is folded or manipulated by darts or gathers
- using templates or ICT; you do not have to be a skilled artist to experiment with different techniques. Using templates allows you to sketch in proportion and scale.

There are three stages of sketching when designing.

1 Sketching initial ideas: these show your thinking and working out of ideas and might include both black and white and colour images and front and back views.

2 Presentation sketches and images: these are more detailed than your initial thoughts and are intended to show your finished ideas. They can be presented as finished coloured sketches with swatches of fabrics and trimmings that may be used for the design, or mixed with a collage of pictures and fabric swatches to form a mood board. You should include both front and back views of the product.

Sketching is an important skill when it comes to presenting your design ideas

3 Technical sketches and illustrations: these show all the technical information that will be used to convert your sketch into 2D patterns; this means including details such as the position of seams and darts.

Your sketches should show how you have met the design specification, so you will need to refer back to your design specification at this stage.

Mood boards

Mood boards are used in two ways: either to focus your mind on possible themes and ideas or as a means of presenting your final ideas. A mood board is a collection of visual information such as sketches, pictures, fabric swatches or anything that catches the theme of the product.

Templates

When sketching ideas, it may be helpful to use templates so that you do not have to keep drawing the same outlines and to help you get scale and sizes right. The main types of templates are:
- fashion templates: these are standard poses and 2D models that you can trace around. They provide the correct scale for sketching garments. Templates for men, women, teenagers and children are available
- templates of different poses: these are standard poses which relate to the type of product that you are sketching. This allows you to trace garment outlines in proportion, as well as developing a range of products.

Using ICT

ICT can be used to make presentation sketches as it enables the designers to show how their products could look. Software programmes are available which show how fabric can be manipulated, designs altered and garment styling developed. A scanner may also be used to incorporate hand-drawn images. This is called computer aided design (CAD).

Activities

1 Choose one of the themes and one of the product areas below and sketch some ideas for a fabric that matches these criteria.
   Themes
   A: the work of a popular artist
   B: young and funky
   C: flowers

   Product areas
   I: clothes – indoors
   II: clothes – outdoors
   III: interiors – bedding

2 Create an A3 page of sketches or use two pages in your sketchbook to show your initial ideas.

Test your knowledge

1 Why do you need to annotate your designs?
2 Why is a fashion template useful when designing clothes?

Coursework

In your coursework portfolio, you will use a range of techniques to develop your ideas; these may include sketching/drawing, photography or illustrations from different media. It is important that you do use of a range of techniques as well as showing your understanding of the use of colour as part of the designing process.

Summary

★ Sketching is a useful tool in the design process as it shows your thinking skills and ideas as well as your knowledge of the initial presentation and technical forms of sketching.

★ Sketching will also gain you marks for communicating your ideas both graphically and through ICT.

Design skills: ICT and CAD

> **In this chapter you will:**
> ★ **learn which ICT tools can be used in designing textiles**
> ★ **learn about CAD.**

The term **ICT** stands for information and communication technology. There are many ways that ICT can be used in textiles to develop and model your design ideas through the use of both software (computer programmes) and hardware (equipment). This can be divided into **CAD** (computer aided design) and **CAM** (computer aided manufacture). Details of CAM will follow later in Chapter 7.12.

Software

Software packages such as Prosketch or Corel Draw will help you to:

- change colourways instantly or demonstrate repeat designs
- change details such as pockets
- create and manipulate patterns or logos for different products
- create fabrics with different textures
- edit your sketches
- use a **database** library of images.

You could use a package such as PowerPoint or Publisher to display your ideas, and spreadsheet packages can be used to work out and show production costs and equipment lists.

Hardware

The use of computer hardware might include the use of:

- a digital camera to show images of your work
- a video camera to show how a garment 'moves' with the model
- a scanner to import sketches into your work
- a printer to print onto paper or onto fabric for design purposes, or to print photos of your work.

Design sketches produced using CAD

Uses of ICT

ICT can be used throughout the design process to:

- communicate – present information in a format that the client or end-user can understand. This might take the form of final presentation drawings, 'flats' (technical drawings), or you might present your research findings in graphs and charts
- generate ideas – create a range of designs and make judgements about whether or not they are appropriate to the product and marketplace
- model ideas – change or develop design ideas, colours and colourings, experiment, or create templates or pattern pieces using pattern generation software
- present ideas – layout of final ideas or specification sheets showing key details that can be passed to other people in order to make the product
- model costs – spreadsheets can be used to model the projected cost of making your product, both singly and in mass production
- model production processes – a flow diagram can model the production line for a product. You will learn more about this in Chapter 7.10.

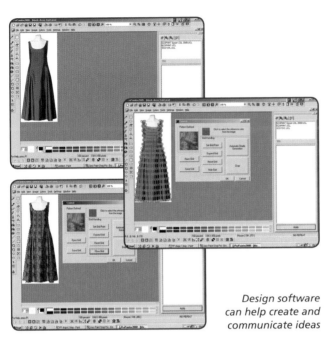

Design software can help create and communicate ideas

Design software

Design software such as ProSketch, Coreldraw, or Techsoft 2D allows you to draw lines and create effects such as texture and shading. It is also good for drawing outlines of images and shapes as the lines can be adapted and controlled with the mouse.

Paint or graphics software

Programmes such as Propainter, Speedstep, Corel Paint, Photoshop and Paintshop Pro allow you to develop patterns and designs. They allow you to change the colour of your design, alter a digital image or create your own textiles patterns.

Design databases

Design software comes with an image database. This provides you with a wide range of ready-made images that can be adapted and changed. The most popular is ClipArt. Specialized programmes such as ProSketch provide a more specialized range of images.

Why do companies use CAD?

Designers are using CAD more and more in their design work as it allows them to adapt and change ideas quickly.

Once a design has been developed using CAD software, it can be produced by CAM equipment, such as computerized embroidery machines, digital printers, cutters or laser cutters.

Overall, in the design and production phase of developing a product, CAD is used to:

- make communication between design and production better – it is easier for all concerned to see how the product is developing
- save money – there is less need for sample making and prototypes as the product can be visualized immediately
- save time and increase productivity – ideas can be visualized quickly and decisions made, so reducing the time it takes to develop the product
- increase creativity – it is more flexible, encourages experimentation, extends the imagination and allows improvements in the development of designs.

Coursework

★ It is important that you show the different ways that you can use ICT in your coursework portfolio, as well as describing how it has helped you in your work.

★ It is also important to explain how industrial ICT processes could be applied to your product. This shows that you are considering how the product could be mass-produced.

Activities

In Chapter 2.5 you were asked to write a design specification for a sports bag. Produce a design for this on a computer and then use CAD to show different colourways. Use annotation to evaluate which colourway is the best in your opinion.

Summary

★ ICT is a key tool in the presentation of your ideas.

★ You can experiment with colour or the layout of your design, moving text and motifs around to find the best result.

★ CAD can be used to save your work and to present your work clearly and concisely.

Project skills

2.9 Modelling skills and product development

In this chapter you will:

★ **learn what modelling skills are and why they are important**

★ **learn what they help you to do.**

What is modelling?

Modelling involves developing and trying out design ideas to see what works best. This can be done either by using a computer or by making a model. Developing a design solution for your project outline is probably the most important section of your coursework. So showing development work, preferably through modelling, is essential for a good grade. In Years 7, 8 and 9 you will have experimented with different ways of creating a product. For example, you might have looked at sample ideas, making small samples, creating a **toile** (a model in paper or cotton calico), experimenting with techniques and manipulating fabric.

In the textile industry, modelling is seen as an important process in the design, development and making of a product as it enables designers to see if the product will work or will need adaptation. Models can also be shown to the client to ensure that they meet their requirements.

Final toile
On my toile I changed the design to make it more interesting. I changed the bottom from one layer with a straight edge to a cross over using two layers. On the top layer there will be a spider web design using silver thread. This is again to add more detail and also to involve the theme of 'gothic'.

The back of the dress was meant to have a zip but I decided to put in a corset style back for three reasons – to make the fit adjustable to make a better fit, to add more detail and also to involve the 'gothic' theme.

A student's toile with annotation

It is important to model your work by making a sample or prototype, as this will help you to see if your 2D designs work in 3D or discover whether you need to make changes to the design. In clothing manufacture, this would be called a toile. It will let you try out your skills, and any equipment or techniques that are new to you, as well as helping you to make decisions about what you are going to do and why. However, you will probably only have time to make one full sample or some small samples of parts of a design.

3D modelling

You could create a sample or prototype product to help you time the processes and decide which processes are the best for you to use. It would also help you to see if the design will work. The model does not have to be full size; you could save time and fabric by making it half size. You create a sample pattern and then make the product or part of the product. You could make a toile out of cheaper fabric. In the fashion industry, the making of the toile is an essential part of the modelling process.

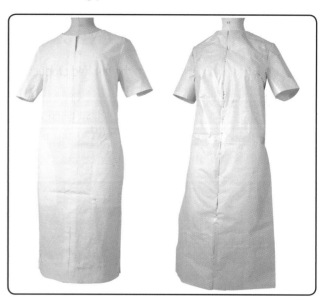

Toiles made of calico (left) and paper (right) are often used in industry to help establish the final shape of a product.

Colour

Experimenting with colour will allow you to see how fabrics react to dyes as well as how the fabric feels and works with the specification. An example of this would be trying dyeing and printing techniques on different fabrics.

Fabric

You can model different fabrics. For example, you can manipulate fabrics using stitch and surface pattern; you can try different types of seams or fabrics to create interest in a design (as well as showing your skills using the sewing machine). You could model gathers, pleats or darts used for shaping. Manipulating fabrics using steam and/or a heat press allows you to test or compare the properties of different fabrics. This will help you to explore how techniques and processes will be incorporated into your product and help you meet the specification.

Using ICT

Using CAD, you can change or develop design ideas, colours and colourings. You can experiment with designs or create templates.

Digital photography is very useful as it allows you to see if your product fits or works and you can see how it looks when it is tried on or used. You could take digital photos of the product and draw on the photographs to show where amendments could be made. Alternatively, you can draw directly on the 'toile' using a fabric pen and then make notes to show how the changes will affect the finished product.

Once you have modelled your ideas, you will need to make a decision about your final product. Are you satisfied with the design as it is or do you need to develop it further? You will need to consider the following questions.

- Do you need to change any elements in your design specification based on what you have found out by modelling the product?
- Does the design brief need to change?
- Do you need to redesign any elements of the design to improve it and, if so, how can this be done?
- Are there any costs involved in making the changes? Do you need to make any changes, such as using different fabrics or components, to ensure you do not go over your budget? Remember that this should be part of your design specification.

Coursework

★ You will probably only have time to make one prototype or toile, but you could try out parts of the design to see how they work.

★ Remember, every time you make a choice or decision, you need to justify it and say why you have made that choice. You will be able to time the processes involved, which will help you produce a production diagram. You could record this in your work diary.

Activities

Use a computer to show how different coloured backgrounds can affect the impression given by a design.

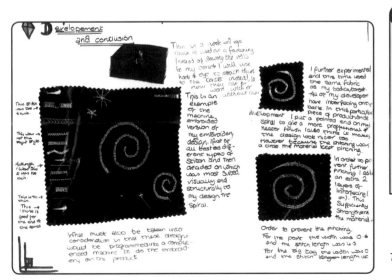

Summary

★ Modelling is really important to enable you to understand how your product works.

★ Modelling allows you to create prototypes or samples, which are important as they provide you with information about the product that you are making.

This a good example of modelling a small sample of fabric.

Project skills

Exam questions

1 Designers will often study existing products before coming up with new ideas for their product. Explain how this can help them. *(6 marks)* (AQA 2004)

2 Describe two ways in which a designer can find information about future trends for denim and denim products. *(4 marks)* (AQA 2004)

3 A designer works to a specification. Give two reasons why a design specification is important. *(2 marks)* (AQA 2003)

4 A national museum is holding a special exhibition to celebrate Native American Indian culture. You are the designer for a manufacturing company. You have been asked to design and make a dressing-up outfit for children.

The outfit must:
• be based on Native American Indian culture
• include a head dress or 3 dimensional feature
• be able to take a reasonable amount of wear and tear
• sell well in a museum shop
• be suitable for small scale production.

You have been asked to show your design ideas. Use the design criteria given in the design brief above.

a Draw and label two different ideas for your product. *(8 marks)*

b Describe two features of the idea you have chosen which will help it to sell. *(4 marks)*

c Use sketches, labelling and notes to present your final design for your product, including the head dress or 3 dimensional feature.

Marks will be awarded for:
• use of theme *(4 marks)*
• originality and quality of design *(10 marks)*
• use of colour in the product *(3 marks)*
• use of fabrics and components *(4 marks)*
• presentation of the final idea *(3 marks)*

d Visitors to the museum want to buy products to remind them of what they have seen. Explain different ways the designers can get ideas from the exhibition. *(4 marks)* (AQA 2005)

Design in society

This section is focused on the impact of textiles in wider society in terms of the following areas:

- cultural and social issues
- historical perspectives
- environmental issues.

You will see that there are many different things to think about when designing textiles products to meet the needs of society.

Design in society

Environmental issues

In this chapter you will:

★ learn about the environmental issues associated with the production of textiles and fashion products

★ learn that environmental issues are concerned with the impact of the production and disposal of textiles and fashion products

★ learn how eco-design is linked to sustainability.

We live in a modern, fast-moving society where there is a high demand for up-to-the-minute products that follow the latest fashions. This means that more and more items are produced to meet this demand. As a result, the production of textiles products has a great impact on the environment.

Impact of textile manufacture on the environment

The effects on the environment of the manufacture of textiles products are varied. The main issues are listed below.

- The **consumption** of **non-renewable** energy resources, such as coal and oil, which cannot be replaced and will eventually run out, causing an energy crisis. The processing of textiles uses non-renewable energy sources and minerals in production and also causes some pollution. Polyester, nylon and acrylic, for example, are made from synthetic fibres that are by-products of oil and take a long time to break down in the environment. Oil and petrol, refined fossil fuels, are used in the transportation of products to their markets.
- Pollution in the air and on the ground. Air and road transport used for transportation of materials, goods and industrial waste emit huge volumes of pollutants into the atmosphere and onto the land. Chemical dyes and printing inks also pollute the environment.
- Damage to and change in the shape of the landscape caused by intensive farming, mining and deforestation.
- Waste management is a growing problem. The production of a textile product creates various forms of waste, from dyes that get into the water system, to paper and card used in packaging. Additionally, the more

Textiles products, such as these dyes, can have a harmful effect on the environment

washing 'care' a product requires, the more harm it could cause from cleaning fluids and detergents.

Important considerations for the textiles industry

Do the methods of textile production harm the environment? Are we using too much electricity or too many chemicals, which could harm our environment? In order to achieve some of the very high performance textiles, it is necessary to use chemical dyes and man-made fibres. Sportswear, for example, often needs to stretch in all directions, be colourfast to withstand frequent washing, and be resistant to weakening through frequent exposure to sweat. Sometimes textiles designers and manufacturers have to make the choice between the performance required of a textile product and the impact of its manufacture on the environment.

Eco-design

Because of this impact on the environment, designers must consider the effect of their product on the environment from the first stages of the design through to the final recycling or disposal of the product. This is called the life cycle of the product. Eco-design involves designing a product with the environment in mind and trying to minimize the damage caused to the environment throughout a product's life cycle.

However, the designer must also produce a product that is acceptable to the client or consumer:

This means that the designer must think about the impact on the environment in the following areas while still designing a product that is acceptable to the client or consumer:

- product planning
- product development
- design process
- functionality
- safety
- ergonomics
- technical issues
- design (aesthetics): how it looks – this is important as many people think that eco-products are not fashionable.

The product life cycle

In order to look at the impact of a product on the environment and its impact on society as a whole, designers will consider the life cycle of a product. They will look at how it can be used from the moment it is designed to the moment it is disposed of. This means thinking about:

- the raw materials – how they are harvested or made
- the production process – how the product is made
- transport and distribution – what is the best method of transport
- uses – how the product will be used by the client or the customer

- recycling – how the product can be recycled and how much of it can be recycled
- care and maintenance – what is needed to look after the product and how can this be made more environmentally friendly
- disposal – how the waste from a product's production can be disposed of and how the product itself can be disposed of at the end of its life. Can it be recycled, will it biodegrade?

❓ Test your knowledge

1 Why is it important for a designer to consider the impact of their designs on the environment?

✏️ Activities

1 Choose a textile or fashion product and create a life cycle chart for it, showing where the product came from and how it was used. You will need to think carefully about its care and maintenance and the possibilities for recycling.

2 Now look at the product again. Could it have been made more environmentally friendly by using different materials or different production methods?

Ⓘⓒ Coursework

You will need to include a section in your coursework showing that you have considered the environmental impact of your final product.

Summary

★ Designers and manufacturers must consider the environment when producing textiles products, but must also make their product appealing to the customer.

Design in society

What designers and manufacturers can do

> **In this chapter you will:**
> ★ learn about new and 'green' fibres and fabrics.

There are strict national and European rules governing the ways in which companies may get rid of waste from production. There are also guidelines to help them to identify the ways in which they can reduce waste and reuse resources. Many leading retail companies now use **social responsibility documents** which contain their guidelines on environmental issues.

Designers and manufacturers can do a number of things to help protect the environment.

Use new fabrics and fibres

Designers now include 'environmentally friendly' products in their designs. They show the consumer that these products not only look good but are of the same quality as traditional products. The Patagonia Fleece, for example, is made from 90 per cent recycled plastic bottles. Patagonia encourages all its customers to 'help the environment by buying only what is needed, wearing it out and passing it on to charities for redistribution'.

The Patagonia Fleece: an example of an 'environmentally friendly' textiles product

Tencel and lyocell

Fibres such as Tencel and lyocell have been designed to have as little effect on the environment as possible. These are modern regenerated fibres used extensively in clothing. Smaller amounts of fossil fuels are used to produce Tencel and lyocell than are used in the manufacture of polyester, and they are also stain and odour resistant. They are made using a 'closed loop' process. This means waste created during manufacture can be reused during the production process.

Ingeo

Ingeo has been developed as another fibre that can replace polyester. It is made from plant starches, which are a renewable resource, and it fully degrades into natural ingredients that add nutrition to the soil. Scientists are also working on developing further fibres based on potatoes and other similar products.

Go 'green'

Designers such as Katherine Hamnett and Conscious Earthwear make clothing that is both fashionable and

Katherine Hamnett clothing

These eco-labels (the Eco-tex standard 100 label and the European eco-label) can be used on environmentally friendly products

wearable and made from fabrics that are organic, recyclable or coloured with vegetable dyes. In some cases, this may mean that that their costs are slightly higher or that they have to accept a different fibre from a sustainable source, such as cotton or wool. They might also consider a range of dye colours from natural sources.

However, some consumers really want high performance man-made fibres including stretch fabrics such as lycra, which may not be available from natural or sustainable sources. In this case, the designer and manufacturer must consider the needs of the consumer and may choose to sacrifice sustainability for performance.

Where a designer has used environmentally friendly 'eco-technology' to produce their garments, they may use an eco-label to advertise the fact.

Conserve resources

It is important that designers protect natural resources. Designers can use fibres and fabrics that come from managed resources, such as managed forests. This means that for every tree cut down, another one is planted. Trees are used in textiles to make regenerated fibres. Tencel is made from wood gathered from sustainable forests. Cotton, linen, wool and silk come from natural sustainable sources.

Manufacturers can also use alternative energy sources, such as wind farms that produce electricity, in the production of textiles products. Designers and manufacturers need to

consider the quantities of fabric and packaging required in the production of a product as well as the processes used in its manufacture. They should constantly strive to reduce the resources used and the amount of waste produced.

Many manufacturers are looking at using 'organic cotton' in their products while organisations such as Traid are launching organic cotton products into the mainstream markets.

Manage waste

Manufacturers now have to follow guidelines on how to get rid of their waste dye and water (**effluent**). To solve the problem of effluent pollution, research is being undertaken into growing fibres with inbuilt colour, such as blue or green cotton. Some companies already use natural dyes, such as vegetable dyes, that are not harmful to the environment or the user.

Coursework

You need to consider the environmental impact of your designs when doing your coursework, but only for the factors that you can control, such as fabric wastage.

Activities

Choose a textiles product and make a list of all the possible factors you could control to protect the environment when designing and manufacturing that product (this activity will also help you with your coursework).

Summary

★ Some textiles and fashion companies have 'environmental' guidelines as part of what is called their 'social responsibility documents'.

★ Manufacturers and designers need to consider how they can help protect the environment by designing and making products that are more environmentally friendly.

Design in society

Recycling textiles

In this chapter you will:

★ **learn about the different ways textiles products, fibres and fabrics can be recycled.**

As our concerns for the environment grow, so does the need to recycle. When producing new textiles products, designers and manufacturers should consider whether their product could be recycled at the end of its life cycle.

The term recycling means to reuse a product, but sometimes before a product can be reused it will need to undergo processing or treatment.

The three main types of recycling are:

- **primary recycling**: second-hand clothing is a form of primary recycling as the item can simply be used again. Many charity shops stock a wide range of recycled textiles products such as bed linen, blankets and clothing
- **secondary recycling** (also called physical recycling): in secondary recycling, the product has to undergo a change before it can be reused. The change will depend on the main fibre of the product. Some products can be left to biodegrade (cellulose such as viscose, cotton and linen); woollen products can be shredded back into fibre form and then respun into yarn; some synthetics, such as nylon, can be melted down and regenerated although this is often of a poorer quality
- **tertiary** or **chemical recycling**: this means breaking down a product and turning it into something else, for example Patagonia Fleece fabric is made from recycled plastic bottles and fabric.

This symbol means the item can be recycled

Methods of recycling

There are companies that specialize in recycling by collecting garments for redistribution or sale, or collecting textiles products to be broken down and then reused. Textile waste is also collected from the manufactures for recycling.

There are various different ways of recycling textiles products.

- Natural fibres can be recycled either into staples for respinning into yarn, or for use in other products.
- Waste silk fibres can be reused to reinforce tyres for racing bikes, or in wadding for performance ski wear.
- Wool garments can be recycled, combined with virgin wool and remade into new garments.
- Traditionally, wool remnants have been recycled and used for wadding in cars and filling for mattresses.
- Linen fibres can be blended with polypropylene fibres to make insulating material, which is recyclable.

The culture of recycling

There has been a long tradition of recycling clothing through second-hand use in the UK. As early as the 1600s, a large trade in second-hand clothing was recorded because of the prohibitive cost of new clothing. Today, there is a strong market for retro or vintage clothing, which may be found in second-hand and charity shops, and is very popular. Many charity shops, such as Scope and Oxfam, also export used clothes to less developed countries. The

Charity shops are a popular method of recycling textiles products

exporting of second-hand clothing is a growing trade; Zambia is one of the largest importers of second-hand clothing. In many of these countries, clothing is brought by the bale and then sold to local dealers who will then distribute it to neighbourhood shops.

However, shops are not the only places to collect unwanted textiles products for recycling. All over the UK, local authorities have set up recycling bins for textiles and clothing products, often in shopping centres and car parks. Garments in good condition may then be redistributed to the needy, exported to other countries, or sent for recycling. Some textiles products are even sent to be made into paper.

The craft of recycling

Recycled textiles products were very popular as far back as the fourteenth century, when the Black Death was sweeping through Europe, because many people could not obtain basic items such as blankets. Instead they would cut up old clothes and then re-sew them into other products, such as blankets. This became known as patchwork and today it is considered to be a very important creative craft.

? Test your knowledge

1 What does the term 'recycling' mean?
2 List three ways in which you can recycle a product.
3 What is secondary recycling?

✎ Activity

Make a list of ten different textiles or fashion products that you have at home. How could you recycle these products?

Summary

★ Recycling products is very important and should be carefully considered by designers and manufacturers of textiles products.

★ It is important to be able to reuse products to lessen the impact on non-renewable resources.

The production of a patchwork blanket

Design in society

3.4 Social and cultural issues in design

Today, we live in a global society. Where textiles products are concerned, this means designing products for different cultures and nationalities who may have different needs. Few designers now cater for only one way of life, as we live in a more multicultural society with a wide range of ethnic types. There are some universal products that can be used by people of any culture, such as T-shirts and jeans. Here, the design of the product will be essentially the same, but the sizing may differ, as people of different races have different body shapes because of the food they eat and their ethnic origins.

Designers are also influenced by designs from different cultures.

Social issues

Social issues in textiles design are related to how we dress and the types of products we wear; this also covers issues concerned with gender, culture and religion.

Clothing is often used to reflect traditional ideas of sexuality and gender. This can be done by colour – for example, few men wear shocking bright pink – or by style, such as the majority of men wearing trousers as opposed to skirts. Some items have become almost unisex over time, such as trousers and t-shirts.

In Africa, fabric designs are often very rich in colour, and many of their fabrics are designed to tell stories or have symbolism. In strict Muslim cultures, on the other hand, clothing is often dark and plain. If you were designing clothing for a strict Muslim culture, you would need to take this into account.

Cultural issues

Many cultures have traditions that are an important part of their identity. These may be linked to the clothes that they wear or to the textiles techniques that they practise. Many of these traditions and crafts are linked to a range of other social practices or events such as early American settlers getting together to sew 'story' quilts telling the story of their family.

Textiles products can also show particular events or tell stories. For instance, the Bayeux Tapestry tells the story of the Battle of Hastings in 1066 and was made soon after the battle (see page 45). In quilt making, stories or symbols can be interwoven in the products that are made.

Traditional techniques

Many traditional techniques and cultural styles have influenced textiles design and manufacture around the world.

- India: cotton is grown in India and is used to make garments. Lavish print and decoration is used and chintz fabrics were developed here.
- China: in traditional Chinese fabrics, silk is often used along with intricate patterns.

Traditional Chinese silk designs

- Indonesia: batik was developed in Indonesia.
- Modern America: new settlers arriving in the New World in the 1600s brought new skills with them. One of the key products that they were well known for is the quilt, which is now a very decorative and sought-after product.
- Scotland: its woven fabrics, tartans, denote tribes or clans.

The role of the designer

When a designer creates a product, he or she has to be aware of the destination market of that product because different cultures have different tastes, needs and ideas about fashion and clothing.

Designers also have to consider the needs of the different groups in each society as they all have specific requirements that will influence the design, such as their:

- gender (male or female)
- age
- traditions (traditional crafts, designs)
- religion (religious ceremonies and prescribed dress)
- allergies (some people are allergic to certain fibres)
- disabilities (designs may need to be adaptable for certain consumers)
- economic status (some people are more affluent than others and therefore prices of products vary).

Designs can be **exclusive** (only be suitable for certain groups or ages) or **inclusive** (suitable to be used by everyone). Designers might also consider 'adaptive' design, which means taking existing products and making them suitable for people who they were not originally intended for. This might, for example, include changing the type of fastenings on clothing to allow for a certain disability.

Coursework

In your coursework, you will design products that meet a range of needs for a range of users. You need to think about whether the product you are creating is well-designed, attractive, functional, and can be used by all possible users.

Test your knowledge

1 Why does a designer need to be aware of different cultures? How does this awareness help them to design a better product?

Activity

A designer has been asked to produce some clothing designs to be sold in Europe and in Africa. Describe how the two ranges would differ in design and in the needs that the fabric would have to meet. Remember to consider the different climates and cultures when thinking about the design.

The Bayeaux Tapestry is an example of a textiles product that shows a particular event

Summary

★ When designing, the designer must consider all aspects of the design process and the market that the product is aimed at.

★ When you design for a particular user group, you have to take into consideration a range of issues, including their tastes and needs.

Design in society

Consumer rights legislation

In this chapter you will:
★ learn about key consumer legislation for textiles products
★ learn about consumer rights.

Consumer rights and responsibilities

When you buy a product, you have rights and responsibilities, and there are laws in place to protect you if things go wrong. **Legislation** means laws and these are provided in the textiles industry to protect the safety and the interests of the consumer. However, the consumer must also understand how the product is to be used and will only be protected by consumer law if they follow the instructions for use. A simple example of this would be a garment that is labelled 'dry clean only'. If the consumer puts it in the washing machine, the manufacturer will not be responsible for the outcome.

Legislation for textiles products

The Trade Descriptions Act

This act states that if a trader tells you something about a product, such as that the fabric is waterproof, then it must be true. All goods must be sold as described.

The Sale of Goods Act

This act requires all products to meet the standard expected of them. They must be of the correct quality and must not be in any way substandard or damaged unless this is pointed out to the customer at the time of purchase. Sometimes goods are sold as damaged or shop-soiled and the price is reduced accordingly. If this is the case, the customer cannot then go back and complain. If goods are sold in this way, the trader will often protect himself or herself by cutting or marking the care label in some way.

All goods must be 'as described' – this relates to the description given by the manufacturer. So a garment described as 'size 12; made from machine washable wool' must meet both of those requirements. The act applies to all goods however they are bought or hired. This includes sale goods unless they are marked as substandard in some way.

The Trade Marks Act

Trademarks are used to protect the manufacturer from copying by other companies and/or individuals. It is also a guarantee to the consumer that they are getting the product that they expect. They are there to protect you from poor quality, cheap imitations and also from high prices being charged for goods of inferior quality.

The Woolmark is a special type of trade mark called a certification trade mark. It can be used under licence by any manufacturer of wool textiles whose products meet The Woolmark Company's high quality specifications

The Trade Marks Act is designed to protect consumers from problems such as counterfeit or cheap imitation products

The Trading Standards Office

This is a government body that looks into the standard and quality of goods offered for sale. Any consumer can ask them to look into a problem if they cannot get their problem resolved by the manufacturer. Trading standards officers check that manufacturers are meeting the legal requirements when making and packaging products, and they do this by taking products apart.

You will also find current information on the Trading Standards website. Go to www.heinemann.co.uk/hotlinks, enter the express code 349XP and click on the link to this chapter.

Maintaining standards

The British Standards Institute (BSI) tests all types of products and awards its kitemark to those that meet the quality required for the product. The manufacturer has to pay for the testing to be carried out by the BSI, which is a non-profit making organization. The BSI will test not only the quality of the end product but also the manufacturing process. If the standard is met, the company can display the kitemark on the packaging and/or labelling of the product. This symbol gives the consumer confidence in the product.

The manufacturer's quality testing system will be checked to make sure it meets the requirements of **ISO 9000**. This includes:

- the way staff are trained
- the way the company checks for quality products
- how the company deals with complaints and how they use these to prevent problems occurring again
- how the company tries to improve its products and manufacturing processes.

Testing usually takes place every six months to ensure the manufacturer is still meeting the standards set by ISO 9000.

The BSI kitemark symbol gives the consumer confidence in the product and a guarantee of safety in the production and use of the product, as long as the instructions for use are correctly followed.

The BSI kitemark

Textiles labelling

All textiles products have a care label giving directions on how to care for the product and the fibre content of the product. This is important, as failure to follow the instructions can remove the consumers' rights for compensation or replacement if the product does not meet expectations. The fibres used have implications for the care of the product, the flammability of the product, and also for the well being of the consumer. For example, some people are allergic to certain fibres. You will learn more about care labelling in Chapter 7.5.

When designing your products, you need to think carefully about what you want the product to do. For example, if you are considering the design for a bag to carry wet swimwear, you must ensure that the fabric is waterproof and colourfast, that the seams are sealed so that they do not leak, and that the bag must retain its strength when wet. If the product meets those requirements, then you should not get complaints from consumers about those issues.

Activity

Imagine you have bought a raincoat from a high street store that was claimed to be 'waterproof'. However, the first time you wear it when it is raining, you are soaked through and the shirt that you are wearing bleeds colour onto the lining of the coat. Who will you complain to and what action would you expect to be taken? Write a letter to the shop manager stating your problem and what you expect them to do.

Summary

★ Consumers are protected by legislation to ensure that the products they buy are up to the standard they require.

★ Consumers have a responsibility to care for the product in the way suggested by the manufacturer.

★ Designers must carefully consider their designs to ensure that their product meets legislative standards and gains consumer approval.

Design in society

Exam questions

1 Denim clothes are often recycled.

  a Give **two** examples of new products which can be made from recycled denim products. *(2 marks)*

  b Give **two** reasons why designers might include recycled products in their designs. *(4 marks)*

    (AQA 2004)

2 Products such as fashion cushions are intended to have a limited life. What are the environmental issues related to the manufacture of such throw away products?

    (4 marks)

    (AQA 2004)

Health and safety

Health and safety is an important aspect to consider when designing both textiles and fashion products. This section looks at health and safety legislation related to the textiles working environment, as you need to be able to work safely on your own and with others around you.

Health and safety also includes looking at the issues to be considered when designing textiles products and the key tests that need to be performed on those products.

What's in this section?

★ **4.1** Health and safety in the workplace

★ **4.2** Health and safety for the product user

★ **4.3** Testing products

4.1 Health and safety in the workplace

In this chapter you will:

★ learn what health and safety in the workplace is

★ learn about risk assessment.

Every employer must ensure that their employees work in a safe environment. To help them do this, they appoint a Health and Safety Officer to make sure that:

- all equipment, machinery, tools and materials are safe to work with; for example, all equipment is safety tested each year and then labelled and dated
- all processes are safe and do not damage the health of employees
- all workers wear suitable, protective clothing
- the actual work environment is safe and healthy; for example, it should not be too noisy or too cold and there should not be trailing cables that people could trip over.

Employees are also responsible for their own health and safety. They must make sure they follow instructions when using equipment and that any action they take does not damage the health and safety of those they are working with. These responsibilities also apply to the work that you do in school.

Manufacturers will put up notices and posters around the workplace to warn of potential dangers and also to inform people where safety equipment, such as the first aid box and the fire extinguisher, is kept. Many will also issue health and safety at work leaflets relevant to their place of work.

Health and safety bodies

In the UK, the Health and Safety Executive (HSE) and the Health and Safety Commission (HSC) are responsible for the rules and regulations that make working environments safe. They also have the power to close down a workplace if they think there are unsafe working practices.

Risk assessment

The Health and Safety at Work Act 1974 was drawn up to protect employees from **hazards** at work. A risk or hazard is a step or process that could cause harm. Everyone has a responsibility to ensure that the way in which they work causes no harm to others; this applies to any working environments you are in.

These hazard and warning signs have become instantly recognizable

STEP 1: Look around the work area for any hazards.

STEP 2: Identify any equipment such as machinery, tools or materials in the work area that could cause a hazard.

STEP 3: Decide who might be harmed by using the equipment and how they might be harmed; for example, a broken needle end left in fabric could injure a worker or a consumer.

STEP 4: List each risk that you find and evaluate the level of risk as high, medium or low. Decide whether the instructions for using the equipment are right or need changing to improve health and safety.

STEP 5: Add a measure to prevent the risk happening; for example, introducing specialist clothing such as masks when handling powdered dye to reduce the risk of allergic or asthmatic reactions.

STEP 6: Every time the equipment you use is changed, review your assessment and revise it if necessary.

The risk assessment checklist

To make sure that you can work safely, a **risk assessment** must be carried out. A risk assessment is a careful examination of what could cause harm to people in the work area. A range of precautions is then identified which prevent anyone getting hurt or ill. All companies, including schools, are legally required to do this, and there are very strict rules for doing so.

A table like the example below could be used to show the risks, controls and actions to prevent hazards in a work situation.

Process	Risk	Control	Remedial action
Cutting out fabric	Scissors cause injury	Scissors need to be suitable for the task; workers should be shown how to use them	Purchase new scissors if needed; retrain workers
	Fabric not cut 'cleanly'	Scissors need to be sharp	Sharpen scissors; check they are appropriate for the fabric
Machining the seams	Sewing through fingers	Train machinists; possibly add finger guard on needle	Retraining; consider the use of a finger guard
	Missed stitches	Replace needle; check that it is the correct type of needle for the fabric, e.g. a ball point needle for stretch fabric	Train staff to look for faults and to choose the correct type of needle
	Unequal seam widths	Use a seam guide	Train staff to use a seam guide
	Tripping over cables	Make sure all cables are safely out of the way	Ensure all cables can be used safely, possibly by using overhead sockets
Pressing the seams out flat	Back injury if the ironing position is too low	Check the height of the ironing position	Adjust the height
	Burns from the iron	Train staff to use the iron; secure rest for the hot iron	Ensure all staff know how to treat burns
	Burning/melting the fabric	Check the temperature required and the iron setting	Adjust thermostat on iron
	Electrical hazards	Check cables and plugs for damage and make sure there is no water in the area	Make sure staff recognize the hazards relating to the use of electricity; have all equipment regularly checked

A textiles company's risk assessment table for making a shirt

Coursework

When producing your plan for manufacture, you should consider health and safety and include evidence of recognizing hazards in the workplace.

Activity

Create a list of equipment that you have used to make a particular product. List the potential hazards or risks associated with this equipment and explain how these risks can be reduced or avoided.

Summary

★ Health and safety is a very important aspect of the work environment. People should be familiar with the rules and regulations governing health and safety.

★ It is important that people are able to work safely and use equipment safely at all times.

Health and safety

In this chapter you will:
★ learn about making textiles products safe for the product user.

All textiles products have to fit in with key health and safety regulations, which ensure that the products are safe to use. To make sure that the products are safe, certain standards and regulations are set for each stage of their manufacture. There is more information about the consumer legislation concerning health and safety in Chapter 3.5.

Safety standards symbols

Safety standards symbols are used to reassure the consumer that their product has been tested by a reputable body to guarantee a certain standard of safety.

The BSI kitemark is one way of showing that a product has met the required safety standards. Many products also carry the **CE mark**. This shows that the product meets the relevant EU (European Union) Directive for safety relating to the product. Safety information should be clearly marked on the product if there might be a risk to the consumer.

Manufacturers should also carry out their own testing, often to the point of destruction, to find possible faults that could occur in order to correct them. These investigations would include testing for quality, such as making sure that the product matches the description given, as well as checking for safety to make sure that there is no danger of anyone being harmed by the product.

In the workplace, the **BEAB** (British Electrotechnical Approvals Board) mark of safety is also used to show that electrical goods have been tested annually to ensure safe working.

The BEAB kitemark

Potential hazards

A hazard is something that can cause harm to the user. Every year there are tragic cases of small children choking on parts of toys or clothing or being harmed by sharp parts of toys. Textiles products such as clothing, bedding and furniture also pose a risk in case of fire, and have to meet strict fire and flammability regulations to protect users.

There are many potential hazards. Some examples of the things that need to be considered when designing and making textiles products are given below.
- Buttons and toggles: these pose a possible choking risk to small children, so if they are used, they must be very securely fastened on. In the case of products for small children, this could be resolved by using poppers or zippers instead.
- Add-on decoration: beading and other decoration must be securely fastened to products so that no loose parts could come off and become a choking hazard.
- Toys for small children, especially those under three years old, must be very carefully tested to ensure there are no parts, like eyes and noses, that could be pulled or chewed off.
- Soft furnishings, upholstery, nightwear and soft toys have to pass stringent flammability tests before they can be accepted as safe.
- The characteristics of the fabric used needs to be considered. For instance, nylon melts when in contact with heat and would not be suitable for insulating material required for, say, oven gloves.

Testing fabrics

To help ensure the health and safety of workers and users, and to guarantee the quality of the end product, fabric testing is carried out. You need to remember that if a claim is made about a product (such as a fabric being flameproof) but not met, the consequences could cause injury or indeed loss of life and could result in legal action.

The testing of textiles products takes place during the following phases of production:
- fibre processing and production
- selection of components such as buttons or zippers
- fabric production

Many toys have a suggested minimum age to warn parents of potential hazards

- garment and product production
- packaging and marketing.

You will learn more about testing in Chapter 4.3.

Activity

Look at a soft toy and make a table of the potential hazards associated with it, along with the steps you would take to prevent these hazards.

[ic] Coursework

Where possible, you should test your product for safety and explain how and why you have done this. For example, you could sew a toggle onto a spare piece of fabric and see how hard it is to pull it off. To test for flammability, you could use the testing cabinet in a science laboratory and, under supervised conditions (using tongs, a fire resistant mat and with water or a fire extinguisher at hand), you could test small pieces of fabric to see how quickly they burn. This MUST be done under controlled supervised conditions and using the fume cupboard, as some fibres (such as acrylics) can give off noxious gases.

Summary

★ Strict testing for the safety of a product gives a guarantee of quality to the consumer and helps protect the manufacturer against claims of injury caused by faulty products.

Health and safety

Testing products

In this chapter you will:
★ learn about tests that can be carried out to ensure the safety of a product
★ learn about tests you can carry out to test your own product.

One way of making sure that textiles products are safe for the user and also that they meet the product specification, is to carry out safety tests. These tests are carried out when making a fabric, when choosing a fabric for a product, throughout the production process and on the finished product. When carrying out these tests, the designer and manufacturer must consider the needs of the intended user.

Possible health and safety tests

There are many tests that can be carried out to ensure health and safety; you can try some of these on your own product to help you choose a fabric or component.

Flammability

Flammability involves testing to see how quickly a fabric will catch fire from a small flame. This would be important for children's nightwear, soft furnishings and upholstery, stage costumes, drapery and soft toys.

Testing at school

See the coursework box in Chapter 4.2 for details on how you could do this test.

Choking

All small parts must be checked to ensure the product is safe for small children to use. In industry, small parts are subjected to rigorous testing to ensure they could not be a choking hazard. Fur and long pile fabrics also need to be tested to ensure that the fibres cannot easily come off, as they could cause a young child to choke.

Testing at school

Simply pull at the pile or toggle and see how easily it comes away.

Allergic reactions

Fur and fur fabrics can give people allergic or asthmatic reactions and need to be checked to ensure the fibres do not come loose too easily. Some dyes may also cause allergic reactions and need to be carefully tested to protect the consumer and the people handling the dyes.

Testing at school

This type of testing cannot easily be done in school.

Quality testing

Insulation

The insulating property of a textile is concerned with preventing heat loss. Insulating fabrics are used for cold weather clothing and bedding. You need to test how well a fabric keeps the user warm. This can easily be done by wrapping a container of hot water with different layers or combinations of fabric. Insert a thermometer in each container and record the temperature at set intervals: the one that takes the longest to cool down is the best insulator.

Testing at school

If your science department has data logging equipment, this could record the temperatures automatically at given intervals of time. This would also add ICT marks to your coursework.

Stain resistance

Stain resistance is concerned with whether the fabric will resist common stains such as tea or coffee. This property in a fabric is useful for upholstery or carpets. If the product cannot easily be cleaned, it may be given a stain resistant finish to improve its quality and durability.

Testing at school

You can take a piece of each fabric and put a variety of stains on it, such as biro, oil, grass, make-up. Wash the fabric normally and see how well the stains come out.

Washability

Washability is concerned with whether the fabric can be washed without losing its shape, shrinking or losing colour.

Testing at school

Cut small, equal-sized squares out of your fabric, then wash and dry them in different ways. Make sure you keep one unwashed square as a control. When all the fabric pieces are dry, compare them for size with your control; this will indicate the washability of the fabric and will also show if it shrinks. This test also links to crease resistance, as it will show how much ironing is required after washing.

Absorbency

The absorbency of a fabric concerns how much water (or perspiration) it can absorb without feeling wet to the touch. This greatly affects the comfort of the fabric and would be used for nightclothes, underwear, bedding and sportswear.

Testing at school

Cut equal-sized strips of fabric and suspend them at the same height over bowls containing the same amount of water. The end of the fabric should be in the water. At regular intervals, record how far up the fabric the water, has progressed. If you add food colouring to the water, it is easier to see. The strip that takes up the most water is the most absorbent fabric.

Abrasion

This test determines how hard wearing a fabric will be to ensure that it will not wear out too soon. It is particularly important for areas of hard wear such as elbows and knees, especially in children's clothing.

Testing at school

Stretch the fabric over a board and secure it. Using a pumice stone or fine sandpaper, rub against the taught fabric. You will need to count the number of strokes and use the same pressure to ensure a fair test of different fabrics. Again, you will need a control piece of unused fabric to compare your test piece against. You will be able to see which is best at resisting wear and tear.

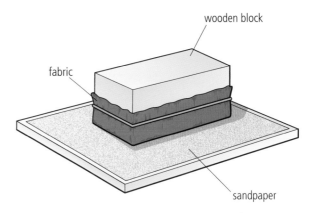

Abrasion testing

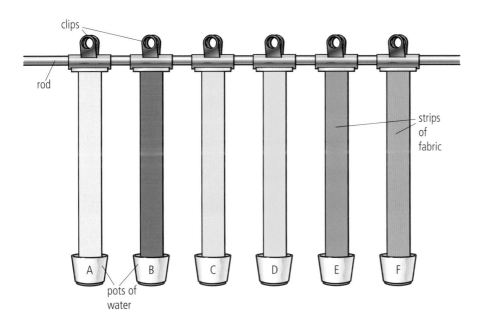

Absorbency testing

Health and safety

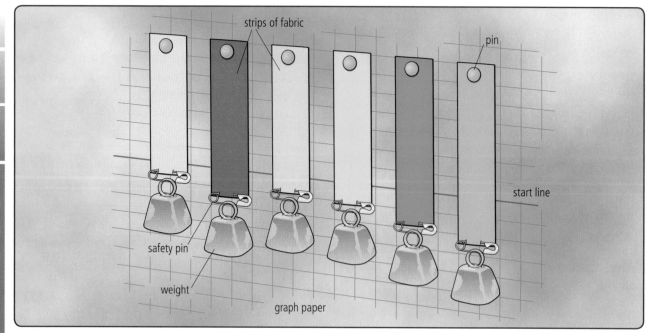

strips of fabric

pin

start line

safety pin

weight

graph paper

Tensile strength testing

Tensile strength (stretch and elasticity)

This test checks the strength of the fabric or fibre but also helps to verify if it will return to its original shape after stretching. This test would be used on climber's ropes, rope ladders, tights and knitwear.

Testing at school

Cut equal-sized strips of the fabrics to be tested and keep a control piece of each. Mark the length of each strip. Hang equal weights onto each strip and suspend at the same height in front of a sheet of graph paper. Leave overnight, if possible, then mark on the graph paper the length that each has reached. Remove the weights and see if they return to their original size.

Colourfastness

Colourfastness is concerned with whether dyes will not wash out or fade in sunlight and is particularly important in clothing and furnishing fabrics.

Testing at school

Cut squares of the fabrics you wish to test; in each case, you will need a square for each test plus a control square.

Sew each square that is to be washed to a square of plain white cotton fabric. (Use large stitches as you will have to unpick them!) Wash squares of each fabric in water at high, medium and low temperatures and possibly using different detergents. When they have dried, unpick the white fabric and check for staining and colour loss against the control. You may want to wash it several times before unpicking and checking.

You can check for sun fading by putting a piece of fabric in a very sunny place and covering half of it with a piece of cardboard. You will need to leave it for some time before lifting the cardboard to see if the exposed piece has faded.

Shower proofing

Showerproofing ensures that light rain will be repelled. Showerproof fabrics are not intended to repel heavy rain and are used for anoraks and jackets.

Waterproofing

Waterproofing ensures that no rain penetrates the fabric. Waterproof fabrics are used for heavy duty raincoats, some sportswear and items such as tents. Remember, the seams would also have to sealed to prevent water penetrating through the stitch holes.

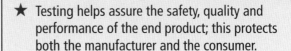

Further information on testing can be found on the BSI website. Go to www.heinemann.co.uk/hotlinks, enter the express code 349XP and click on the link for this chapter.

Coursework

In your textiles coursework, the tests that you could do will be in the manufacture of your product and in the choice of fabric for it. So you could try crushing the fabric in your hand to see if it creases; you could wash a sample to see if it shrinks; or you could test to see how quickly it burns. If you do the burning test, you must use the correct equipment (a clamp, stand and fireproof mat) and you must have a bowl of water to hand. *This test should always be carried out under supervision.* Where possible, you should test against your specification to show how they match. You should keep all samples, then mount and label them to show your results.

Activities

1   From the list of tests, choose the most suitable ones for your product. Pick one of the tests and try it out, recording your results. Try to conduct your test like a science experiment, especially when writing up the results, as this will help your analysis.

2   How has this helped you to decide on your fabric?

Summary

★ Testing helps assure the safety, quality and performance of the end product; this protects both the manufacturer and the consumer.

Health and safety

Exam questions

1 You have been asked to design a product for manufacture. The product must be safe for children to use. Explain two different ways you can ensure your product is safe for children. *(4 marks)*
(AQA 2004)

2 Manufacturers have to make sure that accidents do not happen in the factory. Give three ways in which accidents can be prevented. *(6 marks)*
(AQA 2003)

Fibres and fabrics

This section explores fibres and fabrics. It will enable you to learn how fibres and fabrics are manufactured, discover the key characteristics and properties of these fibres and understand how to make textiles products. From this information you will be able to choose the correct fibres, fabrics, components and equipment required for your project.

What's in this section?

Natural fibres

In this chapter you will:

★ learn what natural fibres are and where they come from

★ learn about the types of natural fibres.

What are fibres?

Fibres form the basis of all textiles products. Fibres are thin, hair-like structures, which can be either short or long. Short fibres are called **staple** fibres and are found in wool and cotton. Long fibres are called **filament** fibres and are found in linen and silk. Long filaments give a smooth finish to fabric, whereas staple fibres have to be spun more tightly to form a yarn and tend to be slightly 'hairier'.

Fibres can come from a natural source or can be man-made. Man-made fibres can be made into staples or filaments; you will learn more about these in Chapters 5.3 and 5.4. A man-made fibre is made from **monomers**, which are joined together to make **polymers**. If you think of monomers as being like beads, then polymers are like a bead necklace.

Fibres have a range of distinct properties and each has its own advantages and disadvantages. When choosing a fibre to make a particular product, it is important to understand what the properties are and how they can contribute to the product, meeting the needs of the brief or the client.

What are natural fibres?

Natural fibres come from a natural source and can be classified as either animal or plant (vegetable) based fibres. The table below shows the sources of natural fibres.

From fibre to fabric

All fibres have to undergo a series of processes to make then into useable yarns and fabrics.

Cotton

Cotton comes from fine hairs attached to the seeds in the ripe seedpod of the cotton plant (called a boll). The cotton is harvested and cleaned to remove any seeds or other matter. It is then dried and repeatedly combed until smooth before being spun into yarn for knitting or weaving into fabric.

Cotton fibres are shaped like a kidney bean or a figure of eight

Wool

Wool comes from the hair of certain animals, grown as protective winter coats. The 'coat' from one animal is known as a fleece. The fleece is shorn from the animal, scoured to clean it and then repeatedly combed until smooth. It can then be spun into yarn for knitting or weaving into fabric.

Animal sources	Fibre	Plant sources	Fibre
Cultivated silkworms	Silk	Cotton (seedpod)	Cotton
Wild silkworms	Silk	Flax	Linen
Sheep	Wool	Sativa plant (stem)	Hemp
Camels	Camel hair	Jute	Jute
Angora goats	Mohair wool		
Kashmir goats	Cashmere wool		

Sources of natural fibres

Wool fibres are unusual because they have overlapping scales and a natural crimp. It is these two factors that can cause wool to shrink if incorrectly washed. In the same way that naturally curly hair will curl more tightly in damp weather, so will the wool fibres when wet. If they are also subjected to friction (rubbing), they will curl more tightly: the scales will hook onto each other and prevent the curls from straightening out again rather like the way that roses or brambles hook together.

Wool fibres are round or oval with scales along the length. Scales help with insulation, but cause problems when fibres are washed. They have a natural crimp

Linen

Linen comes from the stem of the flax plant. The stems are harvested and then soaked in a chemical mixture to allow all the unwanted plant matter to rot away, leaving behind the long fibres. It is then cleaned and dried before being spun into yarn to be knitted or woven. Linen is used mainly for woven fabrics.

Linen fibres are irregular in shape and have ridges like bamboo along the length of the fibre

Silk

Silk comes from the cocoon of the silk moth caterpillar. The caterpillar spins the silk around itself to make the cocoon when it is ready to change into a moth. The cocoons are gathered, washed in hot water to soften and remove the gum that holds them together, then spun into yarn for knitting or weaving. The outer layer of the cocoon produces short staple fibres, but the inside produces very long fine filaments.

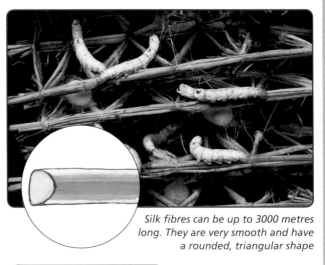

Silk fibres can be up to 3000 metres long. They are very smooth and have a rounded, triangular shape

Coursework

When choosing a fabric to make your product, it is important to understand the properties of the different fibres and how they can contribute to the use of the product to meet the needs of the brief or the client.

Activity

Compare some fibres from each of the four natural fibres described above under a microscope. Draw what you see and describe the differences.

Summary

★ Natural fibres are the oldest type of fibres and they are used for many products.

★ There are two types of fibre: staple and filament.

★ Fibres have to undergo a series of processes to make them into fabric.

Fibres and fabrics

Uses of natural fibres

In this chapter you will:

★ learn about the uses of natural fibres

★ learn about the advantages and disadvantages of natural fibres.

All fibres have different characteristics, advantages and disadvantages. Textiles designers and manufacturers need to know what these are so that the best fibre can be chosen for each product. All natural fibres can be blended with man-made fibres to improve their qualities, such as blending cotton with polyester to reduce creasing. You will learn more about fibre blends and mixes in Chapter 5.5.

Cotton is comfortable and cool to wear and cleans easily, making it an ideal material for warm climates

	Cotton
Physical properties	• Cool to wear • Comfortable next to skin • High absorption of moisture
Aesthetic properties	• Good handle • Strength
Uses	• Clothing (underwear, dresses, shirts, blouses, trousers) • Can be spun into yarn for knitting • Soft furnishings
Fabric names	• Calico • Denim • Gabardine • Terrycloth • Lawn • Muslin
Advantages	• Absorbent • Strong when wet • Durable • Comfortable to wear • Cheaper than linen
Disadvantages	• May crease • Burns easily • Shrinks

Coursework

When doing your coursework project, you will need to consider carefully which materials are most appropriate for your design. Think about the properties, advantages and disadvantages of the materials you research.

Wool	Silk	Linen
• Warm to wear • New 'cool wools' mean that wool can also be cool to wear • Very absorbent • Low flammability • Lambswool and merino are very soft next to skin	• Both warm and cool next to skin • High absorption of moisture • Very comfortable next to the skin because it is so fine and soft	• Cool to wear • High absorption of moisture
• Good handle • Elasticity	• Good handle (feel) • Natural lustre (slight sheen) • Good strength	• Good handle • Strength • Lustre
• Warm clothing • Lightweight wool can be used for dresses and shirts, skirts, trousers, jumpers • Soft furnishings, carpets, blankets	• Silk is expensive so used for luxury goods • Dresses, shirts, blouses, underwear, soft furnishings	• Lightweight clothing (dresses, trousers, shirts, blouses) • Furnishing fabrics, soft furnishings, towels, table linen, sheets
• Felt • Gabardine • Harris tweed	• Chiffon • Damask • Dupion • Shantung • Organza	• Duck • Huckaback
• Warm • Does not crease easily • Comes in a wide range of fabric weights • Comfortable • Produces excellent knitted fabrics	• Soft, lustrous • Drapes well • Can have a wide variety of textures • Easy to print on • Comfortable to wear	• Highly absorbent • Stronger when wet • Durable, smooth finish • Slight sheen • Comfortable to wear • Hard wearing
• May shrink if not washed with care • Can be itchy if worn next to the skin, depending on the type of wool used • Takes a long time to dry	• Expensive • May crease easily • Not always washable	• Creases badly • Can be expensive

Characteristics, advantages and disadvantages of natural fibres

 Activity

Look at the labels in four of the textiles products that you use and see how many natural fibres you can find. Identify which of their properties the product relies on for its success. For example, linen is absorbent and would make a good tea towel.

Summary

★ Natural fibres can be used in many different ways and have a wide range of characteristics. which must be taken into account when designing textiles products.

Fibres and fabrics

Regenerated fibres

In this chapter you will:

★ **learn about regenerated fibres and where they come from**

★ **learn how regenerated fibres are made**

★ **learn about the properties of regenerated fibres.**

What are regenerated fibres?

Regenerated fibres were the first manufactured fibres to be developed. They are **cellulose**-based fibres that originate from plant sources such as the wood from pine trees. Thus, the fibres come from a natural source, but chemicals are used to change the original material, such as wood pulp, into a liquid. This is then forced through small holes and set into filaments. So regenerated fibres are part natural and part man-made.

Types of regenerated fibres

Because they are manufactured fibres, regenerated fibres can be given many different textures. They can be made as either staple or filament fibres, and range from short, crimped staple fibres for spinning into knitting yarn to very fine and silky filament fibres.

The main regenerated fibres are viscose, rayon, acetate, modal, Tencel and lyocell. The newest fibres in this group are Tencel and lyocell, which are more environmentally friendly than some other regenerated fibres because less fossil fuel is used in their production. Tencel and lyocell are made using a 'closed loop' process, which means that waste created during manufacture can be reused during the production process.

How are regenerated fibres made?

Look at the flow chart on page 65 to see a typical regenerated fibre manufacturing process.

Physical properties of regenerated fibres

Because regenerated fibres come from plant sources, their properties are very similar to those of cotton. They are:

- highly absorbent
- very soft and smooth
- comfortable to wear and may have their softness enhanced with a 'peach skin' finish, which means they will drape well
- washable.

As a result, they tend to be used mainly for clothing.

WASH INSIDE OUT
DO NOT RUB STAINS
WASH DEEP COLOURS
TOGETHER
STEAM IRON RECOMMENDED
DO NOT USE
BIOLOGICAL/ENZYME
CONTAINING DETERGENTS
100% LYOCELL

© MARKS AND SPENCER p.l.c
www.marksandspencer.com

F25   0705

MARKS &
SPENCER

machine washable

soft touch
tencel

Tencel is an environmentally friendly man-made fibre that is derived from wood pulp making it luxuriously soft, breathable and easy-to-wear. To keep your Tencel looking and feeling great, please remember to look at the washcare label and follow instructions carefully.

© Marks and Spencer p.l.c.
PO Box 3339 Chester CH99 9QS
ref. AD387 JN15343 A0200

shop online
www.marksandspencer.com

Tencel and lyocell are new regenerated fibres which are now being used in textiles products

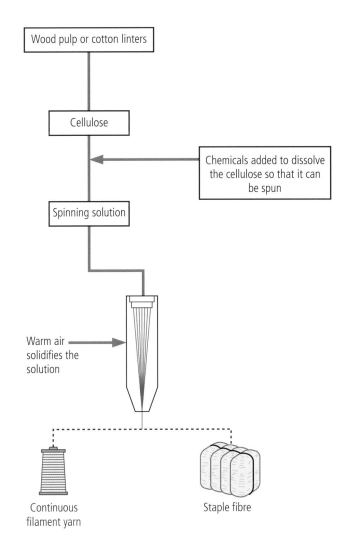

Wood pulp or cotton linters

Cellulose

Chemicals added to dissolve the cellulose so that it can be spun

Spinning solution

Warm air solidifies the solution

Continuous filament yarn

Staple fibre

A typical regenerated fibre manufacturing process

Uses of regenerated fibres

Regenerated fibres can be given different finishes to make them either smooth and shiny or textured. This makes them highly versatile. They can be used in knitted and woven products. They are widely used in textiles and fashion products such as blouses, dresses, lingerie, and ribbons and trimmings.

Coursework

When developing your product ideas, think about the properties, advantages and disadvantages of the different fibres and materials to help you decide which will be most suitable for your design brief.

? Test your knowledge

1 Why would it be more ecologically friendly to use cotton or linen in a product rather than a regenerated fibre?

Summary

★ Regenerated fibres are usually made up of natural cellulose that is chemically treated.

★ Regenerated fibres are soft to the touch and can be combined with other natural fibres, which makes them very versatile.

Fibres and fabrics

Synthetic fibres

In this chapter you will:

★ learn what synthetic fibres are and where they come from

★ learn how synthetic fibres are made

★ learn about the properties of synthetic fibres.

How are synthetic fibres made?

Synthetic fibres are entirely man-made from non-natural sources. Synthetic fibres are made from a synthetic polymer, which comes from oil or other petrol-based chemicals, or from coal. These fibres are made by taking simple chemicals called monomers, and joining them together to create polymers. This process is called polymerization. The mixed polymers are then spun into yarns. Fibres can be blended as they are spun (twisted) into a yarn.

All synthetic fibres belong to groups based on the type of polymer that the fibres are made from. Some of these **generic** groups are polyamide, acrylic and polyester. Different manufacturers may give the fibres a trade name. Each trade name has a capital letter and the symbol ® after it, such as Terylene® and Trevira®. The first synthetic or man-made fibre was polyamide. This was made from oil and coal and given the trade name Nylon®.

Like regenerated fibres, synthetic fibres can be given many different appearances. For example, they can be made as staple or filament fibres and they can be bulked or crimped to give greater volume to the end yarn or fabric. Polyamide and polyester fibres can also be made extremely fine – up to 60 times finer than a human hair – these are known as **microfibres**. Synthetic fibres can also be made to encapsulate chemicals so that, for example, you can have a dishcloth that contains an antibacterial chemical.

Microfibres

Microfibres are very thin hair-like fibres; they are made primarily from either nylon or polyester and can be up to 60 times thinner than human hair. Microfibres are used for all types of textiles products as they are very lightweight, strong, water repellent, good insulators, absorbent, breathable, have a very good handle (feel), drape well and can be given different textured finishes, such as a velvet pile.

The types of products that can be made using microfibres include:
- underwear – absorbent, breathable, soft and lightweight
- hosiery (socks and tights) – lustrous, soft, lightweight
- sportswear – lighter than cotton, protects from the weather, not bulky or heavy, absorbs moisture
- outdoor wear (rainwear) – water repellent and breathable, which helps keep body temperature constant.

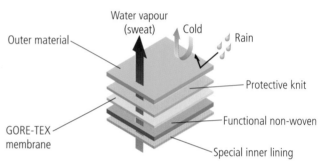

An example of a breathable fabric

Examples of some microfibre fabrics include:
- Meryl Micro® – used for active sportswear
- Clarino® – used as an alternative to leather for fashion garments, bags and shoes
- Tactel Micro® – used for underwear and sportswear.

Thermosetting and thermoplastic properties

Synthetic fibres are unusual in that they have what are called **thermosetting** or **thermoplastic** properties. This allows the fabrics to be manipulated using heat, which softens the fibres and allows the properties of the resulting fabric to be changed. Manufacturers can use this process to add texture to fabrics. For example, the designer Issey Miyake created his 'Pleats Please' range of fabrics by heating the fabric and making the pleats permanent.

Fibre	Trade name	Physical properties	Aesthetic properties	Advantages	Disadvantages	Uses	Microfibre
Polyamide	Nylon	• Very strong • Good elasticity • Thermoplastic • Melts as it burns • Does not decompose (rot) • Resistant to most alkalis and solvents, but damaged by strong acids	• Can be given many different finishes and can be made into microfibres	• Hard wearing and strong • Easy to wash • Inexpensive • Resistant to bacteria and moulds	• Poor absorbency • May be damaged by long-lasting exposure to sunlight, which can cause it to yellow and weaken	• Ropes • Seat belts • Clothing • Carpets	Tactel
Polyester	Terylene	• Very strong both when wet and dry • Flame resistant • Thermoplastic • Good resistance to alkalis and solvents unless very concentrated • Damaged by acids • Does not decompose (rot)	• Can be given a wide variety of finishes and be made into microfibres	• Hard wearing and strong • Inexpensive • Easy to wash • Resistant to moulds and bacteria	• Very poor absorbency	• Most textile uses	Trevira Finesse
Elastane	Lycra	• Very elastic • Lightweight but still strong • Hard wearing • Resistant to biological damage from perspiration • Resistant to chemicals	• Medium to coarse filaments	• Very stretchy and lightweight • Not damaged by sun and sea	• Very poor absorbency	• Swimwear and sportswear	
Acrylic	Courtelle	• Strong but loses strength when wet • Thermoplastic • Shrinks away from heat • Burns slowly and melts	• Fine to coarse staple fibres • Soft	• Can be made soft and warm	• Not very absorbent	• Knitwear and jersey fabrics • Upholstery fabrics	

Properties of synthetic fibres

Activities

1 Look at the garments in your wardrobe. How many are made from regenerated fibres and how many from synthetic fibres? List four reasons why you think this might be.

2 Now suggest other fibres from renewable or sustainable sources that could be used to make these same clothes.

Test your knowledge

List three of the key characteristics of synthetic fibres.

Summary

★ Synthetic fibres are entirely man-made and use up natural resources such as oil and coal.

★ They are very versatile and can be given many different properties.

★ Their properties can be changed using thermosetting.

Fibres and fabrics

Fibre blends and mixes

In this chapter you will:

★ learn about the advantages of fibre blends and mixtures

★ learn what new and smart fibres are.

Fibre mixtures and fibre blends

Different fibres are blended or mixed together in order to utilize the best characteristics of both fibres. For example, cotton is absorbent but tends to crease, whereas polyester does not crease easily but is not very absorbent. By putting the two together, you have an absorbent fabric that does not crease easily.

Fibres can be blended as they are spun (twisted) into a yarn. These yarns can then be used for knitting or weaving. This is called a **fibre blend**. Different yarns made from single fibres can also be mixed when they are woven or knitted. This is called a **fibre mixture**. It would be very difficult indeed to separate the fibres from a blended yarn or fabric, as they are totally integrated together. However, a fibre mix could be separated out again by unravelling the yarns that make up the fabric or the composite yarn.

The main reasons for blending fibres are:
- to improve quality, for example **durability**, comfort or aftercare
- to improve appearance, such as colour or texture
- to increase profitability, for example by mixing or blending an expensive fibre, such as silk, with a cheaper one, such as polyester, the cost can be reduced.

Fibre blends

A fibre blend is made by mixing two or more fibres together before the fibre is spun into a yarn. The most common fibre blend is polyester cotton, but cotton fibres can also be blended with nylon, viscose and modal. They are used in products such as clothing and bedding and give the absorbency and comfort of cotton with the strength of the added fibres.

A blend of wool and nylon is used for products such as carpets, which benefit from the hard wearing qualities of nylon and the natural fire retardant qualities of wool. Fibre

blends that use regenerated fibres, such as viscose and modal, can add softness and create fabrics that are highly absorbent.

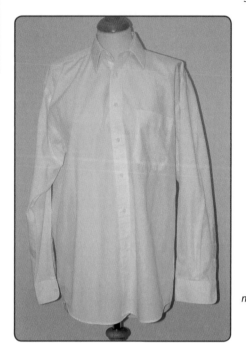

An example of a garment made using fibre blends – in this case, polyester cotton

Fibre mixtures

A fibre mixture or 'union' is a fabric which is made by mixing two or more different yarns: the **weft yarn** (the yarn which goes across the width of the fabric) is one fibre and the **warp yarn** (the yarn which runs the length of the fabric) is a different fibre. Mixing fibres in this way can add additional properties to the fabric. For example, mixing cotton and lycra will produce stretch denim.

Care labelling

Labelling these fabrics is important because each fibre or yarn will have different properties and should therefore be cared for in different ways. It is important to always read the labels on garments. For example, while the cotton in a cotton-lycra mix or blend fabric can be ironed with a hot iron, the lycra cannot, so the lycra element could melt if ironed at the temperature for cotton.

The care label is based on the following factors.
- The proportion of each fibre in the fabric. This is shown in rank order; the fibre with the highest content in the fabric is listed first.

A care label

Levis® Engineered Jeans®

- Natural fibres must be stated using their common names, for example cotton.
- Man-made fibres must be named using their generic names, for example polyamide.

New fibres and fibre blends

A new generation of 'green fibres', which are starch based and come from renewable resources such as sweetcorn and potatoes, have been created, called Tencel. These new fibres have been blended with traditional fibres to create modern fabrics that have new properties and use the best properties of both fibres. An example of this is Levi's® Engineered Jeans®. These twisted jeans combine cotton and tencel fibres to give a strong and durable fabric which helps to hold their twisted shape, but they are also soft and comfortable next to the skin.

? Test your knowledge

1 List three reasons why manufacturers blend or mix fibres, and explain why this makes the fabric better.

Activity

Suggest some blends or mixes of fibres that would work well for sportswear and explain your reasons for choosing them.

Summary

★ Blended and mixed fibres provide designers, manufacturers and users with fabrics that have enhanced properties.

★ New smart fibres provide the user with fabrics that meet the requirements of modern lifestyles.

Fibres and fabrics

Woven fabrics

In this chapter you will:

★ **learn what a woven fabric is**

★ **learn how it is made and used**

★ **learn about the key characteristics of woven fabrics.**

Woven fabrics

If you take a piece of woven fabric and pull at the yarns, they will fray out. You will see that the fabric is made by interlacing two yarns at right angles to each other. The yarns that go horizontally across the fabric are called weft yarns. The yarns that lie vertically in the fabric are called warp yarns and these run the length of the fabric, which is known as the **grain**. The diagonal of the woven fabric is known as the **bias** and the edge of the fabric is finished by the weft yarns wrapping round the warp yarns. This edge is called the **selvedge**.

Weaving is a method of making fabric on a piece of equipment called a weaving loom. A **shuttle loom** is used to create simple plain weaves, a **Jacquard loom** is used to create complex weaves.

Woven fabrics are made using the following processes.

• The yarn is wound on to large bobbins that fit the shuttles used to carry the weft thread from side to side.

• The warp threads are placed on a huge beam. The addition of a sizing (starch solution) makes the yarns smoother and stronger.

• The yarn is then drawn through the heddle. These are fine rods with eyes in them for lifting different threads. This is called drawing.

Types of weave

Plain weave

This is the simplest to construct and gives the tightest method of weaving fabrics. The weft yarn goes over and under alternate warp yarns. The closer the yarns are to each other, the denser the fabric will be. Fabrics such as muslin, taffeta and voile are all plain weave fabrics. It looks the same on both sides and is the cheapest weave to produce.

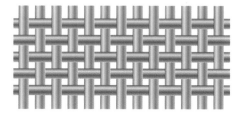

Plain weave

Twill weave

Here, the weft yarn goes over and under more than one warp yarn. The twill weave is recognized by diagonal stripe. The fabrics are soft and can be durable; designs can be varied. Fabrics made using this method are denim, tweed and gabardine. Tartan is a traditional Scottish twill fabric.

Twill weave

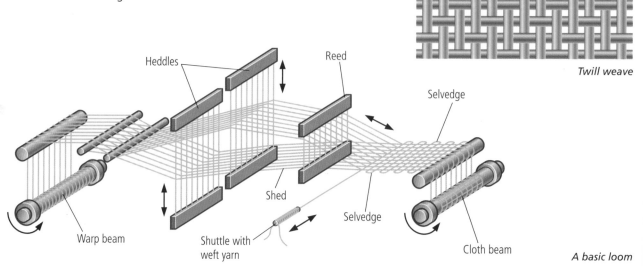

Heddles

Reed

Selvedge

Shed

Selvedge

Warp beam

Shuttle with weft yarn

Cloth beam

A basic loom

Satin or sateen weaves

These are created by a uniform layout of either the warp or the weft yarns. The weft yarns go over one warp yarn then under four or more warp yarns. This layout gives the finished fabric a sheen, but it also snags easily due to the long warp or weft threads, which lie on the surface of the fabric.

These three basic weaves can be altered or combined to produce different fabrics.

Jacquard

Jacquard is the name given to a fabric that has a woven pattern in it. This is created by lifting individual warp threads to create complex patterns. These fabrics are used for furnishings and formal wear. The fabrics are heavy and hard wearing. Jacquard is the name given to fabric that is made on a Jacquard loom and has an all-over fabric design woven into it.

Pile

Pile weaves are woven with an extra layer of weft yarns that form a raised surface. These loops can be cut by running a knife through the loops, and revealing the velvet finish. This is how velvet and corduroy are made. The loops can also be left uncut as in terry towelling. Corduroy is made by weaving the extra weft yarns in lines. Velvet can also be made by weaving two fabrics together and then cutting the yarns between them to make two pieces of fabric. The fabrics made using this method are less hard wearing because they can go 'bald' and are easily crushed. They also have a surface that can absorb moisture.

Pile weave

Honeycombe weave

Honeycombe weaves give heavy textured fabrics, sometimes called waffle fabrics, created by the shortening and lengthening of the warp and weft threads.

Properties of woven fabrics

Woven fabrics have the following properties.
- The side edges, known as selvedges, do not fray unless cut.
- They can be either densely woven or loosely woven (for example, voile, muslin).
- If the fabric is cut anywhere, it will fray.
- The fabric is strongest along the grain of the fabric. The warp yarns are also stronger than the weft yarns as they run the length of the fabric.
- The fabric will stretch on the bias (the diagonal) of the fabric.

CAD/CAM in weaving

CAD and CAM can be used both in the design of the cloth and in the manufacturing of woven cloth. CAD software can be used to create a simulation of a weave or to check a design for colour. The finished fabric can be checked 'virtually' on the screen to ensure that the design works before it is transferred to the loom. At the loom, the designs, colourways and the actual weaving can be changed and controlled using the computer keyboard.

Activities

1 Burberry, a company famous for its woven checked fabric, wants you to create a new woven check for the teenage market. It should have no more than four colours in the warp and four colours in the weft. Create two designs and evaluate them to help you decide which best meets the specification.

2 Find two different types of woven fabric and disassemble them (take them apart) to see how they are made. Record what you find using notes and sketches.

Summary

★ Woven fabrics are created using two interlacing yarns, the weft and the warp, running across and down the length of the fabric.

★ More complex fabrics can be created using weaving methods such as Jacquard.

★ CAD and CAM make the production of woven fabrics easier and quicker.

Fibres and fabrics

Knitted fabrics

In this chapter you will:
★ learn what knitted fabrics are and how they are made
★ learn what knitted fabrics are used for
★ learn about the key characteristics of knitted fabrics.

What is a knitted fabric?

Knitting is an age-old activity, thought to be more than a thousand years old. Knitted fabrics are made up of a range of interlocking loops. The loops run through the fabric and hold the fabric together; if the loops are broken, then the fabric will come apart.

A hand-knitted jumper

There are two types of knitted fabrics: weft knitted and warp knitted.

Weft knit

This can be done by hand, using knitting needles, or by using a machine. The loops run horizontally across the fabric and interlock with the rows above and below (see diagram). If it is done by hand, the pieces of the garment are knitted individually and then joined together. Hand knitting produces individual items such as jumpers, hats and gloves.

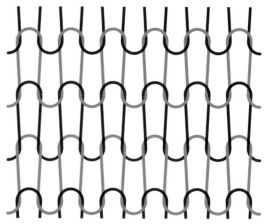

Weft knitted fabric

Weft knitted fabrics can be created on a flat bed machine or a circular knitting machine. Circular machines are popular in factories as they take up less room than flat bed machines and they are faster. Fabric can be made in straight lengths or in tubes, which are useful for items such as socks. It can also be made using short filament yarns and natural or synthetic fibres. Plain knitted weft fabric, known as **single jersey**, is made on a machine. It tends to curl at the edges, which makes it hard to work with. Double jersey is made using two sets of yarn and is thicker so it is more stable, although it is also less stretchy.

Characteristics of weft knitted fabrics

- High elasticity and stretch
- Retains warmth as the loops trap air between them
- It is easy to tell which are the back and the front of the fabric as the top of the loops make horizontal ribs on the back
- Unravels or ladders easily if the fabric is cut or pulled – this means the seams have to be very secure
- Loses its shape very easily

Types of weft knitted fabrics and their uses

- Single jersey: T-shirts, sweaters
- Rib fabric: socks
- Interlock: sportswear
- Fake fur: fur coats, trimmings, shoes
- Pique: sports shirts

Warp knit

Warp knitting is always done using a machine. The loops run the length of the fabric and are linked side by side (see diagram), and the yarns are fed in the direction of the fabric. This type of knitting is like a series of vertical chains and is mostly made using filament yarns.

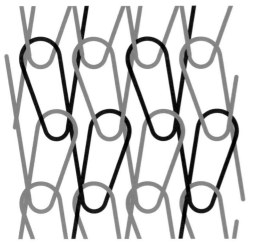

Warp knitted fabric

Characteristics of warp knitted fabrics

- Hard to unravel, so less likely to ladder, which makes it easier to cut and sew
- Faster to produce than weft knitting
- Like all knitted fabrics, it has elasticity, but is able to keep its shape
- It is a very expensive fabric to produce as it takes a long time to set up the machine, which has to be done by hand

Types of warp knitted fabrics and their uses

- Locknit (terry): furnishing fabrics, bed sheets
- Warp knit velour: leisure and sportswear, such as swimming costumes
- Lace and net: bridal wear, fabrics and trimmings
- Fleece: fleece is a warp knitted fabric with extra yarns layered into it and then brushed to produce a napped surface that is soft and raised. Fleece is usually made from polyester fibres and can be double faced, with a nap on both sides, or single faced with a nap on one side.

Knitting and new technology

In recent years, computer aided design (CAD) has enabled the designer to design using simulated stitches. Virtual 3D models of the knitted product can be knitted on screen and any faults can be corrected on screen and adapted. With the use of computer-controlled machines, the knitter or technician is also able to make changes and adaptations to the knitted product as needed via a computer keyboard.

Today, knitting is also used for products other than clothing. One example is in medical products where finely knitted fabrics are used to create heart valves, which can then be implanted into the body. Further advances in knitting technology, using seamless integrated knitting, means that garments can be knitted without seams.

Test your knowledge

1 Name three advantages and three disadvantages of knitted fabrics.

2 Name three different garments that can be knitted and explain why this may be an adavantage.

3 Why might some products be better hand knitted rather than machine knitted?

Activity

Gather together some examples of knitted fabrics. Identify whether they are hand knitted or machine knitted. Use a magnifying glass to see if they are warp or weft knit. Suggest which product each could be used for and explain why it would be suitable.

Summary

★ Knitted fabrics are created either using warp or weft knitting by machine or by hand.

★ Their qualities, such as elasticity and warmth, are used for a wide range of garments and other textiles products.

★ The knitted fabrics of today can be created and seen in 'virtual mode' using CAD and CAM before they are manufactured.

Fibres and fabrics

In this chapter you will:
★ **learn about felted fabrics**
★ **learn about bonded fabrics**
★ **learn about the properties of non-woven fabrics.**

Non-woven fabrics fall into two groups: **bonded** fabrics and **felted** fabrics. In non-woven fabrics, fibres are turned into fabric without first being made into yarn, as is the case with woven and knitted fabrics. Instead they are made by arranging fibres into layers, which face either in one direction or randomly. Layers are then built up to form a web. These have little natural strength so in order to hold the layers and fibres together to make a fabric, they are either felted or bonded.

Felted fabrics

Wool felts

As the name implies, these are made from wool fibres. Wool fibres are short curly staples, which have small scales along their length. When they are treated with heat, moisture and sometimes alkaline chemicals, the fibres curl up – rather like curly hair does in damp weather. The scales prevent the fibres from straightening out again and this causes the wool to shrink in size and felt together. The same thing happens when you wash a wool jumper at a high temperature.

These felts can be moulded into shapes such as hats by using steam. Felts are good insulators, as air is trapped in the web of fibres; they do not fray, and they can be made from recycled wool. They may be used for insulation, collar backs (they can be stitched to hold the shape of a tailored collar), hats, toys and billiard cloths. However, the disadvantage of this fabric is that it is not very strong. Many interior designers use strong industrial felts to design unusual furniture such as floor cushions.

Needle felts

These can be made from almost any fibre. The web of layers is punched through with hot barbed needles that pull the fibres through the fabric to hold it together. Like the wool felts, these fabrics do not fray and they tend to be lighter than wool felts. They are used for interlinings, upholstery, mattress covers and filters.

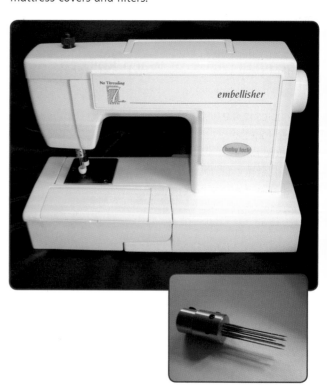

The Babylock Embellisher can perform needle felting by using seven special barbed needles to mesh fabric together

Moulded wool felt hats

Bonded webs

Bonded webs can be made in three ways and are then strengthened to improve their quality.

Dry laid

A web of fibres is laid onto a drum and hot air is pulled through the drum. This softens the fibres, which join together as they are compressed by the air.

Wet laid

These webs are created just like paper. The fibres are mixed with a solvent that softens the fibres. This releases a sticky substance, which glues the fibres together where they touch. They are then laid flat to dry. This gluing process strengthens the bond.

Direct spun

Here, the fibres are spun directly onto a conveyor. This can be done in a random way or an oriented way (crisscrossing over each other). Adhesive (glue) is added to the fibre web by either spraying or dipping, and the web is then pressed to make it stick together.

If the fibres in the web are thermoplastic, they can be bonded together by heating and being pressed together. This could be done all over the fabric or just in places. Bonded fabrics are relatively cheap to produce, they do not fray, and as they are **permeable** (water can pass through them) they can be used as filters. They have no grain and can be cut in any direction, and they have no stretch or give. They do not have much strength and are often strengthened with stitching or gluing.

Uses of bonded webs

Bonded fabrics are used for disposable items such as table linen, underwear, cleaning cloths, and hospital items such as masks and hair coverings. Bonded webs are also useful as interfacings because of their stability and lightness. Some are sewn into place and some are printed with glue so that they can be ironed onto the back of the fabric to

be stiffened. Some are produced as a long strip especially for use on hems. Vilene® is a type of bonded fabric used in interfacing.

Bonded webs can also be used for:
- stabilizers for embroidery work
- soluble stabilizers where you can embroider then wash or iron the stabilizer away leaving a lacy fabric
- interfacing put into garments, such as collars on shirts, to help keep the shape of the garment.

Vilene® interfacing being ironed onto the back of a fabric

Activities

1 Disassemble an old garment and see what types of non-woven fabrics have been used in it. Explain why they would have been used.

2 Use some wool fibres to create a piece of felt that can be used as a needle case.

Summary

★ Felted fabrics and bonded webs are produced without either knitting or weaving.

★ Felts can be moulded into shape using steam.

★ Bonded webs can be used as disposable textiles as well as for interfacing and stabilizing.

Fibres and fabrics

5.9 Smart textiles and interactive textiles

In this chapter you will:

★ learn what smart and interactive textiles are

★ learn about the properties and uses of smart and interactive textiles.

Smart textiles

Smart materials are designed to react to conditions around them, such as heat, light, time and power. They are designed to perform certain functions and are used in many different industries from fashion and furnishing to transport, medicine, construction and the armed forces. Smart materials can:

• sense certain conditions
• sense and react to certain conditions
• sense, react and adapt to certain conditions.

Chromatic textiles

Chromatic textiles are textiles that change colour according to the environment and the wearer. The most well known are the T-shirts by Global Hypercolour, which change colour in response to changes in temperature. Textiles can also be treated to *sense* warmth or cold and then change colour. This function may be used in fashion or may be for more practical purposes such as oven gloves that change colour at a high temperature to warn the wearer of the heat.

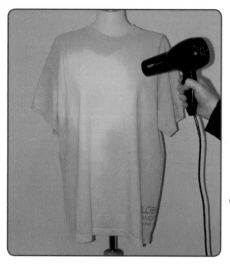

This T-shirt uses chromatic textiles to change colour in response to changes in temperature

Helpful fabrics

Manufacturers are today developing a range of products using fabrics to protect and help us. One example is where fabrics are treated to protect people from the harmful effects of the sun by filtering out ultraviolet rays. Another example of this is using fabrics in pyjamas for babies which sense if the baby stops breathing or their heart stops beating and sound an alarm. This may help to reduce cot deaths.

Micro-encapsulation

Some manufacturers use **micro-encapsulation** to incorporate slow-release chemicals in fabrics to perform a range of functions. This technology is similar to that used for 'scratch and sniff'. Micro-encapsulation is a process where particles of gas, liquids or solids are packaged within a polymer shell. Natural or synthetic fibres can be used. Examples of these modern fabrics are:

• textiles that have scents – many textiles products can now be 'embedded' with perfumes that prevent or mask bad smells (scented socks, sportswear)

• textiles with antibacterial properties – treatments such as Purista can be added to fabrics to give antibacterial qualities. Some babies' clothes and cleaning cloths contain a natural antibacterial called Chitosan. Fabrics can also be imbedded with medicines for medical use

• anti-allergenic textiles – products are added to fabrics to

An example of micro-encapsulation

help prevent allergic reactions to animal hair, pollen or dust mites, for example
- fabrics such as Buzz Off Outdoorwear, which contain a mosquito repellent.

Interactive textiles

Interactive textiles incorporate electronic or conductive fabrics that need a power source to work. The power required can be supplied by a battery, by solar power (the power from the sun) or even through human power. These smart fabrics are used in a whole range of products.
- Nike and Berghaus have both developed jackets that have built-in mobile phone connectors as well as other electronics for the sports enthusiast. Other companies are working on jackets that can have global positioning systems (GPS) embedded in the fabric. These products are being tested in ski resorts to help locate people caught in avalanches.
- The Life Shirt, which can be linked to a computer and be used to monitor blood pressure.
- The newest tagging technology allows the tracking of a garment not only through the manufacturing process but also after the product is bought and then finally disposed of. This tagging will give the retailer more information about the ways in which the product is used and how it is disposed of.
- Gloves that have built-in light emitting diodes (LEDs) that can be switched on or off to allow a cyclist to be seen, or heated mittens to keep people's hands warm.

Signalling textiles

There are textiles products that can help people to be seen, such as reflective yarns. These products contain glass beads within the fabrics, which are reflective only in the dark when a light is shone on them. These could be very useful for cyclists and pedestrians at night. Reflective inks and coatings react to light in the same way.

This jacket, by Berghaus, features a heat-cell panel that is set to two degrees above the core body temperature

? Test your knowledge

1 What is meant by the term 'smart textiles'?

2 Suggest ways in which smart textiles could be useful to you.

3 How might you use interactive textiles?

Activities

1 Using the Internet, the library or the resources in your classroom, spend half an hour researching modern smart fabrics. Try to find out what their properties are and how they might be used.

2 Choose one item of clothing and one soft furnishing item and re-design them to show how they could be improved with the use of smart or interactive textiles.

Summary

★ Smart fabrics react to conditions around them and have many different properties and uses.

★ Textiles are now being developed that can be used for a variety of functions, both useful and decorative, and which incorporate a variety of new and unusual properties.

★ Smart and interactive textiles can be useful in many different industries.

Fibres and fabrics

Printing textiles

> In this chapter you will:
> ★ learn about methods of printing textiles
> ★ learn about using CAD and CAM for printed textiles.

Adding colour to a textile is very important in order to make it appealing and decorative. One of the oldest and most traditional methods of doing this is to print onto the fabric.

Block printing

This is a traditional form of printing. The design is cut out in relief on a wooden, metal or rubber block. This can be done by hand. More often nowadays it is done using a milling machine or a laser cutter. The design is then inked using a roller or by dipping it into the ink or dye. The block is then applied to the fabric and the design is transferred by 'stamping' it onto the fabric. The design can be repeated in different ways. The design of the textile can be varied by painting a background colour onto the fabric or by creating several blocks for a more complex design.

1 Mark the shape on the block

2 cut away the background to raise the design

3 Roll ink onto the block

4 Press the block onto the fabric to create the printed pattern

Traditional block printing

Screen-printing

Screen-printing is sometimes referred to as silk-screen printing and can be done on both a large scale and a small scale. In the classroom, you may use a silk screen combined with a stencil or with an image to block off areas of the screen. A fine mesh is stretched over a wooden frame and the dye is pushed through the screen using a squeegee into the areas that are not blocked off. This method of printing requires a different screen for each colour to be printed.

Flat screen-printing is done in a similar way in industry except each stage is operated by machinery. The designs are transferred to screens using computers, which can separate the colours for each design and reproduce each screen accurately. This method of printing is considered to be cheap for printing large amounts (or runs) of fabric, but it is expensive for doing just a few samples as it can take up to six weeks and cost several thousands of pounds. For this reason, many designers and design companies are using digital printing as the preferred method of producing small runs of designs for sampling.

Engraved roller printing

This is an industrial development from block printing. A series of rollers made of metal have the design photographically engraved on the rollers. Just like

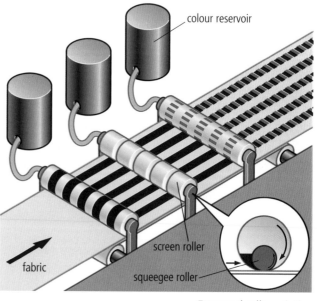

colour reservoir

screen roller

squeegee roller

fabric

Engraved roller printing

screen-printing, there is a separate roller required for each colour and, like screen-printing, this is an expensive method of printing for small runs. It is a very fast method of printing, however, and fabric can be printed at over 250 metres per minute.

Stencilling

This process requires a design to be cut out of card. The design is placed on the fabric and held in place with tape or pins. Using a brush or sponge, the dye is applied to the cut out areas of the design and left to dry. The stencil is then moved to another area of the fabric. More complex stencil designs can be created on the computer and then cut out using a computer controlled cutter such as the stika.

Digital printing

Once a design has been created or modified on the computer (using CAD), it can be sent to the printer to print the design onto the fabric. The design can be transferred to the fabric in a variety of ways depending on the effect that is required. There are two main methods: computer transfer printing and direct printing.

Computer transfer printing

This method of printing uses a computer together with suitable computer software to create the design and then to convey it to a special paper (sublimation paper) that has a coating on it. The design is then transferred to fabric using either a heat press or by ironing. Care has to be taken with designs created using this method as the designs are best washed by hand at 40 °C and not in the washing machine. The designs created can be applied to almost any textile and there are different weights of transfer paper for different fabric types. This works best on fabrics made from synthetic fibres.

Direct printing

Here, the design is printed directly onto the fabric from the computer. The fabric is steamed to fix the design and the **finish** (a thickening agent to make the fabric stiffer while printing) is rinsed from the fabric.

Computer transfer printing

Activities

1 Produce your own design on the computer or scan an existing design into a computer. Print this onto sublimation paper or T-shirt transfer paper and transfer onto fabric. Try this first with a single design and then make the design into a repeat pattern. After you have printed this, try changing the colourways using your computer. Print and then evaluate the results.

2 Experiment with fabric crayons and pens to see which will give a sharper result.

Summary

★ There is a range of printing methods available.

★ The method used will depend on the type of fabric and the quantity of fabric to be printed.

★ Computers can now help with many different types of printing and trial runs.

Fibres and fabrics

Dyeing textiles

In this chapter you will:
★ learn about methods of dyeing textiles.

As well as printing, colour can also be added to fabrics by dipping or immersing the fabric into a dye. Colour can be added either at the fibre or yarn stages of production or to the complete fabric. These stages are called stock dyeing (yarn stage), yarn dyeing (yarn stage) and piece dyeing (completed fabric or finished product). For knitted products, the garment panels are dyed individually or may be printed after construction.

The colour is referred to as the pigment and is 'fixed' using a **mordant**. This is a chemical that makes the dye permanent and helps prevent the colour leaking when the product is cleaned or washed.

Successful dyeing

To apply dye or colour to fabrics or textiles products effectively, the following factors must be taken into consideration.
- The fibre type: not all fibres dye well; natural and regenerated fibres tend to take dye more readily than synthetic fibres.
- The type of product: it is important to ensure that the dyeing method used is right for the style of the product. For example, tie dye would not be right for an Art Deco style cushion.
- The type of dye that is used: some vegetable dyes fade and are not suitable for furnishings as they lose colour when exposed to sunlight.
- The point during the manufacturing process that the dye is applied.
- Testing processes should be in place to check that the dye is uniform across a sample of products taken from the production line.

Transfer dyes and transfer crayons

You might use transfer crayons and paints in school. These are applied to paper and then transferred onto fabric by ironing. Transfer dyes and crayons use a dye called disperse dye, which reacts with heat to transfer from paper to fabric. The heat also sets the dye. This method of printing works best on fabrics with over a 50 per cent synthetic fibre content. Once the dye is applied, the fabric can be used straight away.

Dyeing and resist techniques

Pigment dyeing

This method uses pigment dyes (chemical dyes) that can be applied by immersing the fabric in the dye with the addition of salt. It is a relatively cheap method of applying colour to fabric. Products such as Dylon dye can be used to dye fabrics at home or in the classroom. There are many different Dylon dyes for different fabric types, so you will need to check the information first.

Natural and vegetable dyeing

Many companies are looking at the use of natural and vegetable dyes as an alternative to chemical-based pigment dyes in their effort to be more environmentally friendly. These natural dyes require the addition of a mordant (chemical) that allows the dyes to 'stick' to the fibre molecules. This method of dyeing is not consistent – it is difficult to reproduce the same colour all the time and it is more suitable for natural or regenerated fibres.

Industrial dyeing

In industry, most fabric is piece dyed by one of three methods.
- **Pad** or **continuous** – the fabric goes through a dye bath or through dye pads and is squeezed through rollers

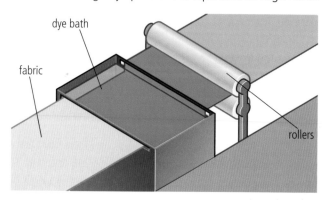

Continuous dyeing

to ensure even penetration of the dye.

- **Semi-continuous** – the fabric passes through dye pads and is held on the roll at a given temperature for several hours.
- **Batch** – a batch of fabric is held in a dyeing machine with the dye. It may be fixed in the same machine.

Manufacturers and designers need to be aware that chemical dyes cause pollution when they are disposed of. As a result, manufacturers have strict guidelines on how they can dispose of such waste.

Producing patterns with dye

Patterns can be made with dyes using **resist** dyeing. Here, a coating, such as wax or a physical barrier such as string, is used to stop the dye being absorbed on certain areas of the fabric.

Batik

Batik originated in the Indonesian island of Java and is now widely practised. Batik uses wax or cassava flour to draw the pattern; this is called the resist.

First, the fabric is stretched over a frame. The resist is then dripped, painted or printed onto the fabric in a pattern. Once the resist has dried, the fabric can be painted with or immersed in dye. As the resist dries, small cracks appear in it, which allow some of the dye through, giving the characteristic crazed background for batik. Batik works well on silk and cotton fabrics.

Batik

Tritik

Tritik is another resist method of dyeing, which uses stitching to prevent the dye reaching areas of the fabric. The design is stitched onto the fabric and then those sections are pulled tight. The dye cannot penetrate the fabric where the stitching pulls it tight. Tritik works well on silk and cotton fabrics.

Tie dye

Tie dye is similar to tritik, but instead of sewing the fabric, it is wrapped, tied or folded in sections to stop the dye penetrating when the fabric is immersed in the dye. To get a multicoloured design, you can untie your fabric once it is dried then retie it and dye it again with a different colour.

Shibori

This technique uses two processes together by either folding or wrapping the fabric and then steaming it. While the fabric is still wrapped, the dye is applied and then the fabric is steamed further to set the dye. When the fabric is unwrapped or unclamped, it retains its sculptural effect. This method was originally used on silk, cotton and lightweight wool.

 Activities

1 Tie or pleat a piece of fabric in several places. Immerse the tied fabric in dye, fix the dye and leave the fabric to dry. Now re-tie or pleat the fabric in a different way and immerse it in a different colour. You will find that the areas that have over-dyed may take colour in different ways according to how tightly they were tied.

2 Compare your results with the rest of the class.

Summary

★ There are different ways of dying fabric depending on the stage of production and the type of fabric.

★ Care needs to be taken to match the type of dyeing or printing with the design, the fibre and the quantity to be processed.

★ Designers and manufacturers need to consider environmental issues when dyeing textiles products.

Fibres and fabrics

In this chapter you will:

★ learn about the processes that can be carried out to improve the performance and appearance of textiles products.

When fabrics have been produced, and before they are made up, they are referred to as **grey goods** (this term also applies to fabrics which have not been dyed or printed). They will go through one or more finishing processes to improve their performance and/or appearance.

Physical finishing

Sometimes also called mechanical finishing, physical finishing is carried out by machinery which is used to change the surface of the fabric; for example, using rollers covered in brushes to give a napped (raised) surface to the fabric.

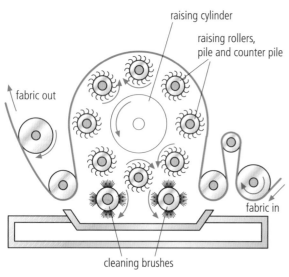

Brushing the surface of a fabric to produce a nap

Biological finishing

This finishing process relies on the naturally occurring bacteria and enzymes that can attack cellulose in fibres. These finishes may be used on cellulose fibres, such as cotton and linen, and on regenerated fibres, such as rayon and lyocell.

Biopolishing takes place before the fabric is dyed. When it is wet, the fabric is treated quickly with enzymes to help remove short fibre ends and make the fabric smoother and less likely to **pill** – to form little bobbles on the surface of the fabric. The enzymes attack the fibres so the process must be stopped quickly by hot washing or even bleaching otherwise the fabric could be damaged or weakened.

Biostoning takes place after dyeing to give a faded look to denim products. To achieve this look the fabric is washed or scoured with pumice stone.

Biostoned jeans

Chemical finishing

There are many different chemical finishes that can be used; examples are given in the table opposite.

Some finishes may need to be washed out before the product is used as it can affect the handle of the fabric – clothing is softer to the touch after washing, towels are more absorbent after washing.

Process	Fabrics treated	Changes made to fabric
Bleaching Natural colour is removed with chemcials	Cotton, linen	Fabric becomes white; can sometimes affect the strength of the fabric
Mercerising Fabric soaked in a solution of sodium hydroxide which makes the fibres swell up and straighten out	Cotton	Fabric is stronger, softer, more shiny and more absorbent
Flame proofing Yarns or fabric soaked in chemicals or sprayed on after other finishing processes	Cotton, linen, rayon	Fabric will resist the spread of flames as it is difficult to ignite. May become stiffer
Water-repellent Silicone applied to prevent water soaking in. Can be applied after other finishes or onto manufactured products	All fabrics	Droplets of water remain on the surface. Air can pass through; if it becomes saturated, water will pass through
Stain resistant Silicone or resins sprayed onto surface	All fabrics	Dirt is prevented from clinging. Care needed when cleaning product
Crease resistant Resin applied and heated to 'cure' it	Cotton, linen, rayon	Fabrics will crease less, but become stiffer. The finish can wash out
Anti-static Chemicals sprayed onto the fabric	Synthetic fibres, acetate, silk	Fabrics made more absorbent, this reduces the build up of static electricity which can attract dust. Fabrics do not 'cling'
Shrink resist Scales on the fibres cause wool to felt. Tips of the scales can be removed using chlorine, or the spaces between them filled in with a thin coating of synthetic resin	Wool	Products labelled as 'machine washable' or 'superwash' have been treated. They can be machine washed on a wool cycle without shrinking

Chemical finishing techniques

Laminated fabrics

Laminated fabrics are created to improve performance and are made by joining two or more fabrics together, rather like a sandwich. They can be bonded together using heat and/or glue. The resulting textile will have the properties of both fabrics. So, for example, a fabric can be both waterproof and breathable, such as Gortex and Sympatex. In these cases, a membrane is sandwiched between two layers of fabric. These fabrics are often used for clothing for extreme sports.

Coated fabrics

A coating is applied to one side only of the fabric. Either a natural or a chemical polymer is applied and then set using heat, or it may be applied to paper and then ironed on. An example of this would be PVC (polyvinylchloride) used to make a fabric waterproof. This is often used for rainwear or aprons. Teflon® may be used to prevent staining in clothing and reflective surfaces could be applied for use in safety clothing.

Activity

Collect and mount some samples of fabric to show three different types of fabric finish. Suggest how they could be used and explain your reasons. You might think about what the benefits of using these finishes are. Think about feel, look, maintenance and cost.

Summary

★ Finishes are applied to fabrics to enhance their performance or appearance.

Fibres and fabrics

Case study: Transprints

In this chapter you will:

★ **learn more about printing designs onto fabric in industry.**

Transprints is a transfer print company based in Morecambe, UK and is a division of Premier Decorative Products Ltd. They have a design office and manufacturing plant in the UK and exhibit at various trade shows to attract customers.

The transfer printing process

Transprints use heat transfer printing, which is the process of transferring a design from paper to fabric using heat. Heat transfer printing was first used in industry in the late 1960s when there was a problem with applying print to polyester, polyester mixes and other man-made fabrics using traditional printing methods. The use of heat made the colours brighter and the design more stable on the new man-made fabrics.

Heat transfer printing allows for intricate and detailed work with delicate colour and tone changes. The development of new and improved man-made fibres and more sophisticated design techniques have seen heat transfer printing grow in popularity. It is used on bags, shoes, sportswear and interior design products.

A product from the Transprints range

The design team

The in-house design team at Transprints create their own designs as well as buying in design ideas from design studios around the world. They also develop customers' own designs to make them suitable for printing. Technology plays a large part in the design process and Transprints' own design team have a sophisticated CAD tool for colour and design manipulation.

Some of the many Transprints designs

Transfer from paper to fabric

Design approval stage

- Using CAD, the artwork is broken down into separate colour files for engraving, which are sent to the client for approval.
- The design is then sent to be engraved onto rollers.
- At the same time, samples of the design are printed to check for colour and, if necessary, sent to the customer for final approval.
- The final design is printed in bulk onto transfer paper.

The use of CAD is crucial in Transprints' design process

The print specification

This is written to give details of the type of fabric to be printed on, the size of the design and repeat patterns, the colours to be used and the quantity of transfer paper to be produced. This will ensure that the pattern is the same every time a fabric is printed.

The transfer printing process has many advantages. It is relatively cheap and easy, it is flexible as it can be used for different fabrics, and there are no chemical wastes for the customer to handle or dispose of, which makes it environmentally friendly.

Transferring designs from CAD onto the fabric

The designs are separated into different colours using a CAD system. Each colour will be printed using a different roller. When designs are agreed, they are engraved onto special rollers by one of these methods.

Gravure

The designs are engraved on to steel-based, copperplated rollers. Using up to six cylinders (one cylinder per colour), it is possible to achieve great subtlety in terms of colour gradation. Gravure works particularly well when printing fine tones, textures and sophisticated details.

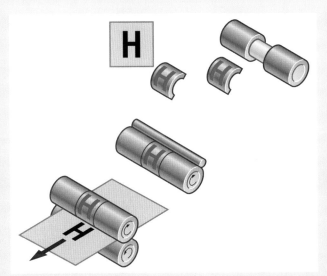

The gravure process

Flexographic

This is only suitable for designs that are made up of two colours. Here, the designs are printed onto rollers made of rubber, using two cylinders per design (one cylinder per colour). This method is ideal for solid and simple tone work. Flexographic printing is the classic method used for basic designs such as spots and stripes.

Once the design is engraved onto the roller, it can then be printed onto special transfer paper using disperse dyes. Transprints then sends the client their printed paper for them to print their fabric. This is done by passing both paper and fabric over a large heated roller at the correct temperature and pressure. This transfers the design from paper to fabric by a process called sublimation, where the dyes change from solid to gas without becoming liquid. The equipment used to do this is called a transfer printing calendar.

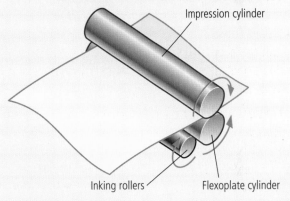

Impression cylinder

Inking rollers

Flexoplate cylinder

The flexography process

Activity

Look closely at a printed design and work out how many colour rollers have been used; remember that where one colour overlaps with another, the colour may change. For example, if you print red over yellow, you may end up with orange; if you print yellow over red, the shade of orange may well be different.

Summary

★ CAD is an ideal tool to use for designing for printing.

★ The print can then be carried out using CAM to fully automate the process.

Fibres and fabrics

Exam questions

1 You are a textile product designer. You have to design a denim product for children aged 5 to 10 years old. Choose **one** of the following:

either

A a textile product for a child's room

or

B an item of clothing for a child.

  a Denim fabrics are usually made from cotton. Give three reasons why denim is a good fabric to use for your product. *(6 marks)*

  b Denim fabric is woven. The picture below shows a twill weave.

    Give two reasons for using a twill weave. *(4 marks)*

                               (AQA 2004)

6 Making textiles products

This section is about the processes needed to make your product. It will enable you to construct, shape, manipulate and decorate textiles in various ways. From the information in this section you will aslo be able to match the correct components and fastenings with the fabrics, tools, equipment and processes that you may use to ensure high levels of quality and safety.

What's in this section?

Constructing textiles: seams

> **In this chapter you will:**
> ★ learn how fabrics can be joined together.

Seams

A **seam** is a means of joining two pieces of fabric together. The manufacturing specification will give the seam allowance – how far the seam should be machined from the edge of the fabric (usually 1.5 cm but often narrower in industry). It will include the details of the specific tolerances for each process so that the quality control checks can be met. The **tolerance** is the small amount of variance allowed on each process, so a seam allowance may be set at 1.5 cm with a tolerance of +/– 0.1 mm. The **manufacturing specification** will also list the type of seam to be used, the needle size and type, and the thread type.

In most seams, the right sides of the fabric are placed with the edges level and are then pinned and tacked by hand before being machine stitched. The pins should be placed at right angles to the edge of the fabric to prevent the fabric from being distorted.

All seams should be well pressed at each stage of making or they will not lie flat.

Equipment

The equipment needed to carry out the processes of joining fabric together includes:

- a sewing machine to join and neaten the seams
- an iron, an ironing board and possibly a sleeve board (which is like a mini ironing board and will fit inside a sleeve)
- a thick, heat-reflecting pad or ironing board cover to absorb steam and prevent seam lines from showing when pressed
- a needle board for pressing velvet
- a tailor's ham with a variety of different curves on it for pressing awkward surfaces such as sleeve heads.

Sleeve board

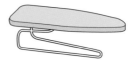

The sleeve board is for pressing tubular items.

Underlay

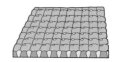

Special heat reflecting pads, or simple felt materials can be used as underlays for pressing. They spread the pressure and absorb the steam.

Press mitt

Hand-held pads are a useful aid in top pressing garments which are difficult to lay flat.

Needle bed

Needle beds are helpful when dealing with sensitive pile fabrics (velvet).

Some equipment that can be used as pressing aids

Plain seams

Plain seams are the most common way of joining two pieces of fabric. These avoid bulk and can be used on many different materials. The seams will need neatening if the product is not to be lined, as the raw edges will fray.

Methods of neatening seams

- Pinking with pinking shears if the weave is very firm.
- **Overlocking** to join and neaten the seams
- Zigzag with a domestic machine, either on each side separately or by pressing both sides of the seam to the same side and sewing together. The thickness of the cloth would determine which method to use.
- Using bias binding to edge both sides of the seam.

Overlocking

The most common means of neatening seams in industry is by using the overlocker. This is a machine that uses three or more threads at a time; it trims the seam and at the same time sews over the cut edge, enclosing the edges. Some overlockers will sew the seam at the same time as neatening it. There is also a wide variety of domestic overlockers available.

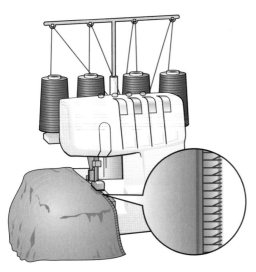

Domestic overlocker

Curved and angled seams

In order to make a successful curved or angled seam, it is necessary to clip into the curve. This enables the seam to be turned to the right side without unsightly pulling or puckering.

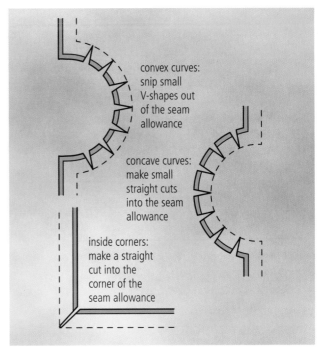

convex curves: snip small V-shapes out of the seam allowance

concave curves: make small straight cuts into the seam allowance

inside corners: make a straight cut into the corner of the seam allowance

Curved and angled seams

French seam

French seams are used for very fine fabrics and lingerie, and completely enclose the raw edges of the fabric.

Double-machined seam

A double-machined seam is particularly strong, very flat and also decorative. It is commonly used on jeans and where a flat finish is needed.

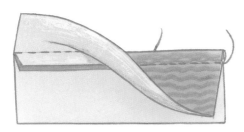

French and double-machined seams

Activities

1 Try making the seams shown here on different types of fabric.

2 Look at what you are wearing. How many types of seams can you identify?

Coursework

You should explain why you have chosen to use a particular seam or method of neatening. You should include some sample seams in your folder to show why you made your final choice.

Summary

★ To achieve a good result, a seam must be evenly sewn using the correct thread, needle size and type, the appropriate style of seam and neatening for the fabric and the product.

Making textiles products

6.2 Adding shape to textiles products

In this chapter you will:

★ learn about adding shape and structure to a product

★ learn how to finish an edge.

Very few textiles products are created to fit a flat shape, which means that the flat fabric must be shaped to fit. There are several ways of doing this.

Gathers

Gathers are created by making two rows of stitches approximately 0.25 cm apart. They can be made using a long machine stitch with a loosened upper tension, or by making small, evenly placed running stitches. In either case, the stitches are fastened at one end leaving the other free to be gently pulled up, gathering the fabric. This may be used anywhere the fabric needs to be taken in and gives a rounded effect.

Gathers

Pleats

Pleats are folds in the fabric that are stitched into place. Sometimes they are sewn all they way down the fold. There are three types of pleat: knife pleats, box pleats and inverted pleats. These are used for taking in fullness and adding shape.

  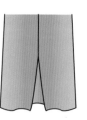

Pleats

Pin tucks

Pin tucks are small folds of fabric sewn down their length and pressed to one side. Sometimes they are used to take in fullness but more often are added for decoration on clothing or other products such as cushions.

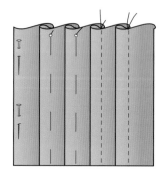

Pin tucks

Darts

Darts are made by folding the fabric and then sewing it in place. They are used to make a garment fit closely and are usually found at the bust or waist of a garment or sometimes at the elbow of a fitted sleeve. Darts are intended to be inconspicuous and should be pressed towards the sides of a garment or downwards at the bust; this means they will lie flatter against the curve of the body.

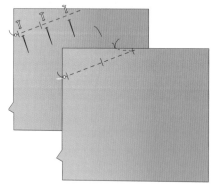

Darts

Giving structure to a garment

In order for most garments to look good, they need extra structure to help them. Some of the ways this can be done include:

- lining: this gives a neat finish and the extra layer inside the garment helps it to hang well. It also increases the level of comfort for the wearer
- interfacing: this is where an extra layer of stiffer fabric is used to give shape and stability to a garment, such as with collars, cuffs and waistbands. The interlining is cut to the same shape as the fabric. Interlinings can be sew-in or iron-in (fusible) and come in a range of different weaves and weights to suit different fabrics. They are also available as an unwoven fabric that has no grain and is therefore very economical to use
- interlining: this is similar to interfacing. Interlining is generally added between the lining and main fabric to add warmth
- shoulder pads: these are used to add styling detail and slight padding to the shoulder line.

Finishing an edge

If a finished garment is to look good and wear well, all the edges must be finished suitably. Some of the possible finishes include:

- hems – used to finish and weight the lower edge of a garment. There are several ways of doing this depending on the weight of the fabric and the style of the garment
- facings – these are made using additional material cut to the same shape as the garment edge. These are usually sewn to the right side of the garment and then turned through to give a neat and stable edge; occasionally they are applied the other way round to form a decorative feature
- collars and cuffs – these are style features that are used to finish the neck and sleeve edges
- waistbands – these are interfaced bands used to neaten and strengthen the waist of a garment and to prevent stretching
- binding – these are made from strips of fabric and are used to cover raw edges. They can be cut from the same fabric or a contrasting fabric and can be used to replace

any of the other finishes, though perhaps not giving as firm a result. To cover a curved edge, these need to be cut on the bias (bias binding).

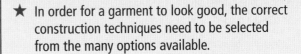

Coursework

If you are using a commercial pattern, make sure that you transfer all the pattern markings carefully and note any parts that need lining, interlining or interfacing.

Test your knowledge

1 Why do we need to add shape to a garment?
2 Where might you use a dart and why would you choose it?
3 Describe the difference between knife pleats and pin tucks.

Activities

Make a set of samples of gathers, pleats, pin tucks and darts.

Summary

★ In order for a garment to look good, the correct construction techniques need to be selected from the many options available.

★ You need to consider the style of the garment as well as the type and weight of the fabric.

Making textiles products

Manipulating textiles

Textiles and fashion designers **manipulate** fabrics to make textiles products. This means they handle them in order to change flat fabrics into shaped products. They might do this by using folding or stitching the fabric, or by applying heat or chemicals, or by using a combination of these practices. To manipulate textiles, it is important to understand the properties of the fibres and fabrics you are using.

Physical manipulation of fabrics

In clothing, the main ways of manipulating fabrics are by using **pleats/tucks**, **darts**, and **gathers**, which change the flat two-dimensional fabric into a three-dimensional product. The darts and pleats can be further changed using machine stitching.

Pleats and tucks

Pleats and tucks are folds of fabric held in place by stitching. A pleat is where the folds are stitched along their fold edge. If this stitching is only where the folds join

The same garment can be manipulated in different ways to give different effects

another piece of fabric, this is a tuck. Pleats and tucks are used in garments to reduce fullness or to create decorative effects, such as in the kilt. Jennie Rayment has done a lot of work showing how calico can be used in this way. Her book *Creative Tucks and Texture for Quilters and Embroiderers* is a useful source of information.

Darts

Darts are commonly used in clothing as they provide a way of changing the shape of the fabric and making a garment fit more closely. There are different types of darts: straight, curved, single or double ended. They can also be used in a decorative way to create 'funky' 3D shapes that can be used on garments on the right side of the fabric or in a radiating fan of small darts.

Gathers

Using gathers reduces fullness by using small stitches that can be pulled up to reduce the length of the fabric. This can be done by machine or by hand.

Shirring elastic can also be used to create unusual effects. The shirring elastic is put in the bobbin, the machine is threaded as normal. When the fabric is removed from the machine, the elastic will contract, leaving a gathered textured fabric.

Smocking is a traditional craft and another method of reducing fullness. The gathering can be done by hand, using a pleater, or by using a sewing machine. The gathers then have surface embroidery worked over them, which holds the gathers and forms a decoration.

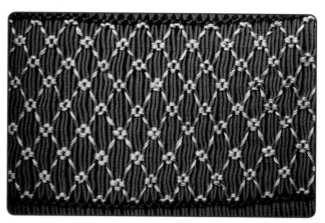

Smocking

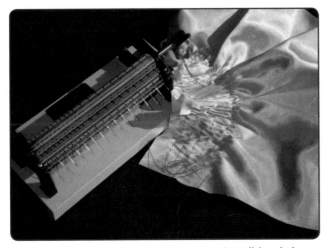
A traditional pleater

Manipulating fabrics to give a textured effect

Along with quilting, **cording** can also be used to give a textured effect to fabrics. Cording is the process of trapping a cord between two layers of fabric then securing it using stitching. This can be done by hand or with a sewing machine where you would use a twin needle to trap the cord. It gives the finished surface of your product a three-dimensional textured surface effect and can be used on garments or in furnishing.

? Test your knowledge

1 Name three ways in which fabrics can be manipulated to reduce fullness.

2 Why might you want to manipulate the fabric? Give three reasons.

3 How can heat help to manipulate fabric?

✎ Activity

Use a piece of calico and try, using pleats or tucks, to make a decorative panel for the front of a bag. Evaluate how well this has succeeded and work out how much extra fabric you need to allow for the pleats and tucks.

Coursework

Try pleating or manipulating a piece of your fabric to see if it could be used for decorative effect.

Manipulating fabrics using heat

Fabrics can also be manipulated using steam or by using the thermoplastic (melting) or thermosetting (memory) properties of certain fibres.

When manipulating textiles fabrics using heat, it is important to understand the properties of the fibres and fabrics you are using. Different fibres react to heat or water, for example, in different ways. Wool and acrylic fabrics can be manipulated by boiling or washing in hot soapy water. The agitation will cause the fibres to felt. Once dry, the finished fabrics can be cut without fraying. This process enables you to create unique fabrics that can be shaped easily as they are produced, such as when making hats.

Synthetic fibres, such as nylon and polyester, react to steam or dry heat, which can set pleats of folds in the fabric. You can also create textured effects on lightweight polyester and chiffon fabrics by tying up the fabric just as you would when tie dyeing. The fabrics are then steamed and left to dry. When they are unravelled they hold the shape of the way they were tied as the heat has set the shape.

Many contemporary designers use a combination of modern and new techniques to create a range of unique fabrics.

Summary

★ Fabrics can be shaped by using stitches or by using heat.

★ Knowing about the properties of fibres and fabrics can help the designer to create unusual products with shape and texture.

Making textiles products

Issey Miyake: Pleats Please

In this chapter you will:

★ learn how pleats can be used to shape and decorate.

Pleats Please

Issey Miyake is one of the foremost present-day textiles designers. He was born in Hiroshima, Japan, in 1938 and grew up in the aftermath of the nuclear bomb that fell on Hiroshima in 1945. He entered the European fashion scene in the early 1970s and revolutionized it with his creative and innovative fabrics and designs. He founded the Miyake Design Studio in 1970 to further his work.

Pleats Please was introduced in 1993 and makes use of lightweight permanently pleated fabrics. This echoes the work of Mariano Fortuny and his Delphos dresses in 1910; the significant difference being that Fortuny used silk as his fabric of choice while Miyake uses modern polyester to give permanent pleating.

Making the pleats

In the 1970s, Issey Miyake began experimenting with a 'flat piece of cloth' design based on the concept of the flat planes of the kimono, but he developed it further by adding pleats. Traditionally, pleated products are made by pleating the fabric and then cutting and sewing it together. Issey Miyake's garments are cut to three times the required size and, after they have been made up, the pleats are applied by heat-pressing the fabric between sheets of paper by a machine. The pleats can also be made to run in different directions because of the hand finish, giving an unusual texture. Because the fibre is 100 per cent polyester and thermoplastic, the pleats are permanent. The fabric and paper have to be hand fed into the machine, making this a very expensive and labour-intensive process.

The Delphos dress

A coat designed by Issey Myake

This process developed into Pleats Please, a range of more comfortable garments carrying printed designs like the simple one-piece dress shown. The pleats made the garments cling to the body and move with it.

While the process of making the clothes is labour intensive, the care of the finished product is not. The clothes are practical and functional. They are machine washable, non-iron, quick drying and crush-resistant for packing. The shapes used are very simple but the colours and prints are wide-ranging and easily changed for each passing season. They are rather like wearing a piece of art.

A one-piece dress by Issey Myake

Activities

1 Take two pieces of fine polyester fabric and place them one at a time between two pieces of baking parchment. Fold the fabric and parchment into pleats and press with a hot iron. Unwrap the fabric carefully and see how the pleats have set. This process can also be carried out by placing the fabrics in a hot oven (120°C) for 30 minutes. Safety point: the fabric will be very hot.

2 Join the two pieces together. Is this easy to do? What effect does the pleating have on the finish of the seam?

3 Now try joining two pieces of the unpleated fabric together and then pleating the seamed fabric. Which gives a better result?

4 How could you make use of the pleating properties in a garment?

Summary

★ Pleats add interest and texture as well as taking in excess fullness.

Making textiles products

Decorating and enhancing textiles

In this chapter you will:

★ **learn how to add surface texture and decoration to textiles**

★ **learn how to choose the appropriate method to add decoration.**

Fabrics and products can be decorated to improve their look and feel in many ways. The key methods of adding decoration and enhancement to fabrics are:

- stitching and **embroidery**
- **appliqué**
- **patchwork**
- beads and sequins.

Stitching and embroidery

This provides a flat surface and is washable. There are several means of stiching and embroidering.

- Hand stitching and embroidery – creating a design in stitches and threads – are time consuming and are suitable only for small areas.
- Freehand machine stitching, where the foot is removed and the fabric guided by hand, is more suitable for larger areas of fabric or larger designs.

- Computer embroidered machine stitching: decorative patterns can be programmed into the sewing machine; it only requires threading.
- Computerized stitching: this uses the preset function on the machine for pattern mirroring, resetting the start of a pattern to match existing patterns, and using stitch counters to automatically match for you.

You can also create added texture to embroidered products by layering different types of fabrics and stitching into them, or by painting or printing onto fabric then adding textured machine stitching or patterns.

Appliqué

Appliqué is a technique of decorating fabric by combining fabrics in an interesting pattern and applying them to a background. Appliqué can be sewn in place or, in some cases, glued. The design is cut up so the pieces provide a template to use for cutting out the fabric to be appliquéd. This is placed in position, then hand or machine sewn into place. This is quick to do and very effective.

An embroidery machine

An example of Appliqué

Patchwork

Patchwork is a technique of creating pattern or new fabric with leftover fabrics. It was popularized by the early North American settlers who used it to make quilts. Women traditionally created patchwork in groups, with each person completing a section. This not only provided the women with a social gathering but also made good use of whatever fabric was available. It also meant that the quilt was finished far more quickly with several people working together. When these products were first made they were inexpensive, as they made use of fabric scraps and old garments, but today these antique quilts can cost hundreds or even thousands of pounds.

The fabrics are cut into geometric shapes and then sewn together by hand to create a pattern, often tessellating like mathematical patterns. The designs can be flipped or mirrored and often have names like tumbling blocks. Patchwork can either be flat or have a padded backing added and quilted. It is effective and colourful and can also be quick if a sewing machine is used.

Quilting

Patchwork, appliqué and embroidery can be made more textural by **quilting**. Quilting is the process of sandwiching a soft cotton wool-like padding (batting) between two layers of fabric, then stitching through it to create a textured surface. Quilting is used on clothing, bedding and furnishing products. The batting traps air and so adds warmth to the product.

Beads and sequins

These may be hand sewn in place to add decoration and texture; in some cases, it is possible to machine sew sequin strips in place. Beads and sequins are raised from the surface of the fabric and are delicate. They are usually applied to areas where they will not get too much wear, which could damage them. Beads and sequins are an expensive form of decoration.

Devoré

Devoré involves printing a mixed fabric, such as viscose and silk, with a chemical. This chemical takes away the silk or the viscose in that section leaving a design in relief and a fine gauze in between. This is a costly process most often used for small areas.

> **✎ Activity**
>
> Using a selection of different fabrics, make a 30 cm by 30 cm patchwork square, which could be used to decorate the front of either a cushion or a bag. Once you have made the patchwork, decorate it using the most appropriate method for the fabric. State why you have chosen this method.

> **Summary**
>
> ★ Adding texture to fabrics can enhance the way a fabric looks and feels.
>
> ★ Care should be taken to use fabrics of similiar weight and strength for appliqué and patchwork products – this makes the fabric care easier.

stitching   batting

fabric bottom

fabric top

Quilting

6.6 Using a sewing machine to decorate textiles

In this chapter you will:

★ learn about using the sewing machine to create surface design

★ learn about using a computerized embroidery sewing machine for CAD/CAM.

Ordinary sewing machines and computerized sewing machines can be used not only to join fabrics together but also to create decorative finishes.

Machine embroidery

Using the existing stitches on the sewing machine, it is possible to create different effects by changing the length or width of the stitches and by layering them, possibly using different colours or shades of thread.

You can also use **free form embroidery** stitching using **satin stitch** or straight stitch. Free form embroidery allows you to decide in which direction the stitching will go and how it will look because it is sewn using an embroidery ring and not the presser foot. You can overlay stitches and colours. You can develop your design by painting or adding dyes to the fabric before stitching begins.

Computerized sewing machines

Computerized sewing machines are an example of CAM and they can be programmed to sew in many different ways.

• To carry out repetitive operations, such as producing buttonholes, where they all need to be identical.

• To produce lines of pattern stitching from the sewing machine's memory and start each line at the beginning of the pattern.

• To stitch a motif or logo from the sewing machine's memory bank or database.

• To stitch a motif or logo that has been designed on the computer or scanned into it and the information transferred to the sewing machine.

You can use computer aided design (CAD) to create a design before stitching. For this you need either a sewing machine with a built-in computer screen or the sewing machine needs to be linked to a separate computer. This is done by a direct link from the computer or by a special card that can be put into a **card reader** and then fed into the sewing machine. The card lets you change your design into stitch format, this is called digitizing, and you will be able to select your own choice of stitches.

Many manufacturers have digitized designs on their websites that can be downloaded.

Using CAD to develop decorative embroidered products

Creating decorative textiles

To develop decorative embroidered products using CAD or CAM, you will need the following:

- the design that you are going to stitch
- a scanner for scanning artwork into the computer
- digitizing or conversion software to convert your design from artwork to stitch format
- **stabilizer or interfacing,** which will help to create a firm base for the embroidery. Some fabrics stretch and distort when embroidered; a stabilizer will help to keep the fabric stable and will stop the embroidery from causing distortion. Stabilizers are available in soluble (dissolvable) and non-soluble form, in different weights for different types of fabric and in iron-on and sew-in forms. For a lightweight silk, you would need a much finer stabilizer than for denim. You also need to check if your fabric is washable before deciding which to use as some stabilizers do not wash well. You will also need to experiment with iron-on and sew-in versions – sometimes on fine fabrics the iron-on stabilizers make the finished work look too stiff
- **machine embroidery thread** – this can either be made of silk, viscose, rayon, or low twist polyester. You will not get good results from ordinary sewing thread; it is not as fine and does not have the same sheen as machine embroidery thread. Embroidery threads have greater twist
- fine machine needles
- an embroidery ring or frame to hold your fabric taut while it is being sewn
- the correct machine foot, which has a space underneath it to allow for the embroidery and will not snag on the raised surface
- samples of the fabric to be used for the final product – if you do not use the actual fabric, you will not get a true result.

Coursework

An embroidered sample, designed on the computer and made using a computerized sewing machine, would give you good evidence of CAD and CAM for your folder (as long as it is relevant to your project).

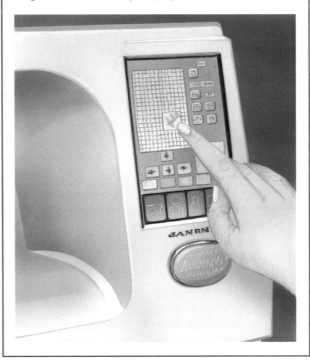

Activity

Experiment with a sewing machine to create a piece of free style embroidery that would be suitable for a bag. If you have the software to do this using CAD, then you should do so, and use either an embroidery machine or a computerized machine to carry it out.

Summary

★ The sewing machine is a versatile tool and can be used to create different effects.

★ A computerized embroidery machine allows you to easily produce repetitive processes and allows designs to be created and transferred to fabric quickly.

★ Through computerized embroidery you can easily experiment with style, stitches and colour.

Making textiles products

6.7 Components in textiles

In this chapter you will:

★ learn about matching components with the fabrics, tools, equipment and processes that are used to ensure the best possible outcome in terms of quality and safety.

Components

Components are the items that you will need to help you complete your work. Components that you buy ready-made, such as Velcro and zip fasteners, are known as **pre-manufactured components**. It is important to choose these carefully so that they fit the quality of the product and the weight of fabric that you are using. For example, if you have made a velvet jacket, it would look better with a high quality button rather than a cheap plastic one. If you are selecting a zip fastener for a chiffon skirt, it would be better to choose a lightweight nylon zip rather than a metal jeans zip.

When choosing a component, it is important that its properties match the properties of the end product. For example, if the end product is washable, then the components used must also be washable. If the product can be tumble-dried, the components must not melt in the heat from the drier.

Safety issues

Another major consideration when selecting components is safety. The choice of components must not compromise the safety of the end product. For example, if you are making products for small children, they should not have buttons or beads that could be chewed off and present a choking hazard. Likewise, if you have used flame resistant fabric for stage costumes, all the components used must also be flame resistant otherwise a seam sewn with flammable thread could spread flames through a flame resistant fabric. You can now purchase flame resistant spray that can be added to interior products.

Components are used to:
• add strength
• open and close a product
• add protection
• add decoration
• insulate
• add shape or mould a product.

The table opposite shows some of the many components you could use.

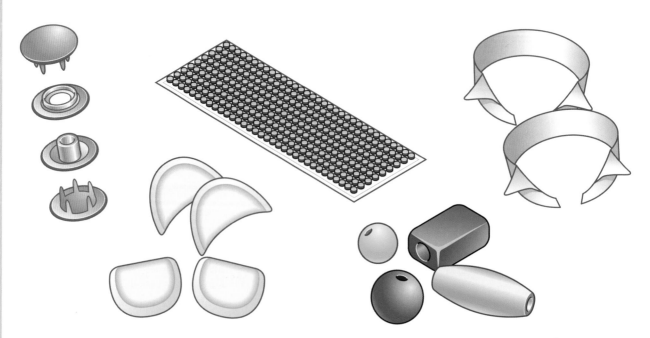

Some components

Component	Function	Reason for choice
Sewing thread	• To hold the product together • Possibly for decoration or to accent a particular feature	• Cotton thread for cotton fabric • Thicker thread for accenting
Buttons, toggles	• To close the product	• Appropriate for the product, the right size and decorative
Zip fastener	• To provide a closure	• Flat, neat method of fastening, could be open ended
Beads	• To provide a focal point • To catch the light	• Washable, easily attached and easily available
Rigilene boning	• To stiffen and support the fabric, for example in a basque or strapless dress	• This type of boning is washable and easy to use
Pre-manufactured collars and cuffs	• To reduce making time and reduce the difficulty of making • To replace worn collars and cuffs	• This greatly reduces making time • Could be used to change the style of an existing garment and give it a new look
Velcro (hook and loop fastening)	• To provide a closure that is easy to manage. This could help children or people who find small fastenings difficult to manage	• Velcro is only suitable for robust fabrics that will not snag easily
Braid	• For decoration	• The weight and style of the braid needs to be chosen to complement the item to be decorated
Press fasteners, hooks and eyes	• Alternative methods of closure	• Both give a flat closure and could be decorative • Press fasteners are easy to open
Shoulder pads	• To slightly pad the shoulders and give a squarer look	• Foam pads selected as they are washable

Functions of components

Producing component parts

Technology plays a part in the manufacture of textile components. Many components are made using CAD and CAM. The components can be made on a large scale and the use of computerized equipment ensures that the components are all the same size and quality. Different qualities and quantities of component can be manufactured to suit different qualities of product. Thus a cheap end product would use cheap mass-produced components and a couture product would use components specifically made for that product.

Coursework

You could include a table like the one below in your coursework to show the components that you have used.

Activity

As a group activity, take an old garment and disassemble it. Identify how and why different components have been used in the manufacture of the product.

Summary

★ Most textiles manufacturers make use of pre-manufactured components to speed up manufacture and reduce the skills base needed for production.

★ The quality of the components can greatly add to the quality of the end product.

★ It is important to bear safety issues in mind when choosing components.

Making textiles products

6.8 Types of fastenings

> **In this chapter you will:**
> ★ learn about different types of closures.

There are many different ways of closing and fastening textiles products so it is important to think about the function of the product before deciding on the type of closure. For example, a heavy duty nylon zip fastener would be a good closure for a tent made from heavy waterproof fabric, but it would not be appropriate for the closure of an evening gown because it would be too heavy. Some products require fastenings to be very durable, whereas others need to be invisible.

When choosing fastenings, you need to think about these factors.
- Who will be using the product?
- Does the fastening need to be invisible?
- Is it a design feature?
- How much will the fastening cost?
- How secure does it need to be?

Zip fasteners

These are available in several different weights to suit different types of fabric. They also come in many different lengths. Zips can be made of nylon which is washable. They range from very lightweight to chunky open-ended zippers, which may have a decorative finish. You can even find them set with diamante! Jeans zips tend to be slightly curved and made of metal.

Concealed zips are available and are often used in bought garments. They are more difficult to put in neatly and you may need a special attachment for the sewing machine in order to do this.

Zips are a popular type of fastening

Zips can be applied either as a decorative feature or as a discreet closure. They are suitable for most closures, but great care must be taken to select the correct type and colour for the product and fabric.

Buttons and toggles

Buttons and toggles come in a wide variety of sizes and styles, from small plastic shirt buttons and novelty buttons for children to very expensive custom-made buttons for couture garments. Buttons can be decorative as well as functional. It is said that the quality of the buttons can make or break a garment. It is certainly worth taking the time to select the right button for the product, and it is worth investing in high quality buttons for high quality products. You should also ensure that the buttons have the same care instructions as the garment. For example, you should not put buttons on a dry clean only product that will dissolve in the cleaning solvent!

When selecting the buttons, you also need to think about the buttonholes. The buttonholes need to be slightly larger than the button and may be hand or machine worked.

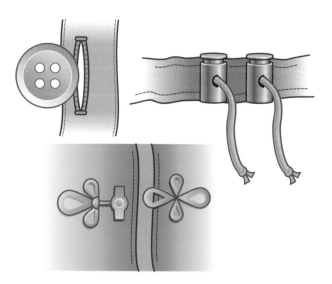

Buttons and toggles

Press-studs

Sometimes called press fasteners or poppers, these provide a flat closure. The two circular pieces are attached to the fabric using thread, and they snap together to join the edges. They again come in a wide variety of sizes and types, from the tiny transparent plastic ones suitable for a very discreet closure to large metal ones on jeans and jackets. Again, care needs to be taken to match the press-studs with the purpose of the product and the fabric used.

Press studs

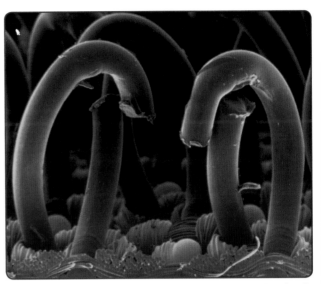

Magnified velcro hooks

Hooks and eyes

These are often made of metal and come in many sizes; they are also available as hook and eye tape that can be machined in place. They are most commonly used at the top of garments and in underwear and corsetry to provide a strong flat closure that will not pop open. They are attached using thread.

Activity

Compare the results achieved using a zip, buttons and velcro for a jacket front opening. Which would you choose and why?

Summary

★ The type of closure you choose must take into account the purpose of the product, the user and the quality of finish required.

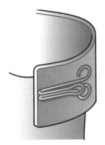 

Hooks and eyes

Velcro

Velcro is a useful fastening for anyone who finds standard fastenings fiddly and difficult; it only needs to be pressed together. Velcro is made up of tape with fine nylon hooks on one side and a soft looped fabric on the other, and the hooks simply stick to the loops. It works well for robust fabrics, but the hooks can snag fine fabrics. Velcro is quite heavy and bulky even in its lightest form, which is another reason why it is unsuitable for fine fabrics. If used in a very long closure, it may open under pressure. Velcro is washable and hard

Making textiles products

6.9 Equipment in textiles

In this chapter you will:

★ **learn about matching materials and components with tools, equipment and processes**

★ **learn about matching techniques, processes and equipment to the product**

★ **learn to identify the correct materials, components, tools and equipment and use them safely and correctly.**

The materials and tools used in textiles manufacture include the fabrics, the components needed to complete the product, and the tools such as scissors and sewing machines needed to construct the product.

Tools and equipment

Tools and equipment include any item that you use to help you make the product. They need to be chosen with care in order to make the task easier to carry out. You need to select the most appropriate equipment for the fabric you are using. For example, choosing the right type of scissors

Equipment	Function	Reason for choice
Hand sewing needles • Betweens • Sharps • Crewel • Ball point • Leather points • Machine needles (these can also be ball point or leather point)	• Short needles for quilting • General hand sewing • Embroidery • Used for stretch fabrics • Bladed ends for sewing leather • Used in sewing machines	• The short needles are easier to make stabbing stitches when quilting • Longer needles for stitching along the fabric • Large eyed to carry thicker threads • They penetrate the fabric better • They cut through the leather, caution they leave holes • The appropriate needle needs to be chosen for the type of fabric, such as ball points for stretch fabric or fine needles for chiffon
Measuring tape	To measure accurately	This should be made of non-stretch fabric and clearly marked in cm or both cm and inches. It should have metal ends so that it cannot fray
Unpicker	Used to unpick hand and machine stitches and to cut button holes	It should have a sharp point and a good cutting edge; it should only be used for fabric
Tailor's chalk	Used to transfer markings onto fabric	The marks are not permanent and will brush out easily
Tracing wheel/carbon paper	Used to transfer markings onto fabric	The tracing wheel leaves a very fine line and the carbon washes out easily
Embroidery ring	Used for both hand and machine embroidery to hold the fabric taut	In order that the fabric does not pucker when sewn, especially with longer stitches
Craft knife	Used for cutting stencils	Should have a retractable blade for safety
Cutting table	Large table for cutting fabric	Big enough to take the width of the fabric
• Scissors • Pinking shears • Small sharp scissors	• To cut fabric • Neaten fabric • Snip threads and buttonholes	• Long shears for even cuts • They give a zigzag cut that does not fray very easily • Short sharp blades for small controlled cuts
Pins	To hold fabric in place for cutting or sewing	Pins are fine and sharp and will not mark your fabric
Sewing machine	To sew the fabric together	Faster and stronger than hand sewing
Overlocker	To neaten seams	Gives a professional finish

Functions of different equipment

will make the task easier and give a better result. If you cut fabric with paper scissors, you will find that the fabric will not cut cleanly.

The table opposite shows you a range of equipment used in textiles manufacturing and reasons why each might be chosen.

Processes

A **process** is any step taken in the making of a product, such as adding pattern or colour to the fabric, sewing up the seams, or pressing the final product. The table below shows the processes involved in making a bag, along with the function of each process and the reason for choosing that particular process

Process	Function	Reason for choice
Digitally print the image onto the front panel of the bag	To decorate and identify ownership	Quick, easy and uses CAD/CAM
Join the side seams of the bag with an open seam	To hold it together	The open seam is very flat
Neaten the seams with the overlocker	To prevent the fabric from fraying	It gives a professional finish and simulates industry
Press the seam	To flatten the seam	It improves the finished appearance

An example of the processes involved in making a bag

 **Activity**

Compile a table, similar to the one above, showing the processes involved in making an everyday textiles product such as a pair of trousers. Include the functions of the processes and your reasons for choosing each particular process.

Summary

★ It is important to use the correct materials, components, tools and equipment when making textile products in order to make a safe, well-manufactured quality product.

★ Knowing how the equipment works and how components and processes can be used together is an important part of the design process.

Examples of basic textiles equipment

Making textiles products

Exam questions

1 Fastenings on a product are important. Look at the products below.

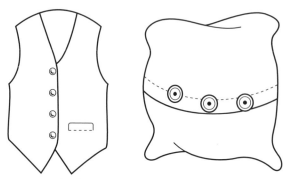

  a Name the fastenings used. *(1 mark)*

  b Name one different fastening that could be used.
   (1 mark)

  c Give two reasons for your choice. *(2 marks)*
  (AQA 2004)

2 Some denim products have decorated edges as a feature. Sketch **two** suitable edge features you have researched.

(4 marks)
(AQA 2004)

3 A designer has chosen to use a full length zip on the outside of their bag.

  a Name **one** other fastening that could have been used instead. *(1 mark)*

  b Explain why you think the zip was chosen *(3 marks)*
  (AQA 2003)

7 Industrial processes and practices

This section explores the industrial practices used in textile manufacture. You will learn how these industrial practices and processes work and why they are used.

What's in this section?

Industrial processes and practices

Production systems

In this chapter you will:
★ learn about different systems of production.

A **system** is the means used to manage the way a product is produced. It is a series of three interacting stages.

INPUT ➡ PROCESS ➡ OUTPUT

The three stages of a system

A system is designed for each different product and includes all the checks and feedback loops to ensure a quality product is made efficiently. This, in turn, helps to make the product cost effective. A good system will ensure the production runs smoothly.

There are many different types of textiles products, and so there are many different methods of producing these. Manufacturers must decide which is the best method for producing their product. One important factor in this decision is the number to be produced. The four main types of production systems are:

- **one-off production**
- batch production
- mass production
- line production.

One-off production

One-off production is when a product is made by one person, or only one is made – it is not mass-produced. When you make your textiles product in the classroom, you are carrying out one-off production. This is also known as individual, job or **bespoke** production.

Haute couture is an example of limited edition, one-off production. These garments are made by skilled machinists and workers and have a great deal of handwork. They are made of expensive fabrics and are of limited production. Examples of this type of garment are seen every year in the fashion catwalk shows. Often the garments are too extreme for everyday use but act as a showcase for the designer and attracts clients who will order similar but slightly more wearable versions. Very few people can afford this type of designer wear. The garments are exquisitely made but very expensive.

A haute couture designer and some of his designs

Batch production

Batch production is a method of production which produces a fixed number of identical products. Products that are produced to meet a particular demand or for a particular part of the season are batch produced. When the garments have been sold, they are not reordered and a different product will replace them.

This is a relatively inexpensive production system, as it is simple and flexible. It can easily be modified and is most commonly used for fashion items that change rapidly. The number produced can be varied to meet demand.

Mass or volume production

This refers to large-scale production, usually using a production line. Large numbers of identical products are made using this method. It is used for products that are in continuous demand such as school trousers. It is the cheapest system to run as fabric and components can be bought in bulk and large numbers can be made quickly. It is also the best way of meeting a large demand.

The work is passed along the production line from operator to operator so that each consecutive task can be completed. In this case, the production line is the line of machinists working on the product. This may also be called the **progressive bundle system** because of the way the bundles (all the pieces of the product) are sent along the production line. Mass production can be divided into the following categories.

part of the expense of a production system is in shutting down and starting up machinery. It may also involve the use of computer aided manufacturing, as in the long run machinery is cheaper than people.

The progressive bundle system

Mass production

Synchronized or straight-line production

Each worker or operator does the same task over and over again, each time passing the product over to the next operator in the production line. The task should always take the same amount of time so that the production line can be synchronized. The worker becomes skilled and quick at this task, so helping to speed up production. This is suitable for producing large numbers of products for large retailers. However, this may become very boring for the operators, and they may not be able to transfer to a different task very easily.

Repetitive flow production

This type of mass production system uses semi-skilled operators, who will perform specific tasks in the production of a product. Repetitive flow production is made up of a range of sub-assembly lines that concentrate on one particular aspect of the production process. It is possible for this to be fully or semi-automated (some of the sub-assembly lines can be automated where others cannot) and it produces large quantities of identical products at low cost.

Continual flow production

This system runs for 24 hours a day until the product is complete. It is used for producing products that are simple in design and have a limited number of components. It is also used where products need to be made cheaply, as

Activity

Explain which system would be appropriate for making each of the following and give clear reasons for your choices.
- a school shirt
- a winter coat
- a cushion.

Coursework

You will be using a one-off system to produce your coursework, but you could consider the way that your product may need to be adapted if it were to go into mass production. For example, if you have used hand embroidery to decorate your product, you may consider using an industrial CAM embroidery machine for mass production, or you may print the design instead, which would considerably reduce the manufacturing costs.

Summary

★ Manufacturers need to choose the right manufacturing system for the products that are being made.

Industrial processes and practices

Modifying textiles products

In this chapter you will:

★ **learn what it means to modify textiles products**

★ **learn why textiles products might be modified.**

What is modifying?

The word 'modify' means to change. Modifying a textile product means to change and therefore improve it. **Modifications** can be very simple, such as changing the colour of the fabric or the finished size of the product, or they could be quite complex, such as adding tiered frills to a plain skirt. Often modifications are made to make the product match the design brief more closely, or to ensure it can be made to budget.

Why are designs modified?

Modifications are part of the design and production process and can take place at any stage in the production where it is found that a change will improve either the finished product or the way it is to be produced. Most modifications relate to the following:

• size or fit
• fabric type
• colour
• trimmings
• components, for example threads, buttons, interlining
• cost – the product may be too expensive to produce on a large scale
• the production method – if it is too long, it may be too expensive
• the availability of the right specialist equipment to make the product
• the decorative techniques used on the product
• the type of stitching to be used.

Using samples

One way of finding out whether a product needs to be modified is to make a sample. When making a clothing product, for example, a design team will make two sample garments (also known as **toiles**). These are either made from cotton calico or a similar weight fabric to the one being used.

One sample is for the production team to use as a guide to see how the product is to be made. This sample is usually measured on a workroom stand or tailor's dummy and uses anthropometric measurement data based on the client target group. This is more accurate and is the model that is used for modifying the product. The production team can check that the production processes are correct for the design and that the product can be made within budget. This will tell them whether any modifications need to be made to the design or manufacturing process.

The other sample is for the buyers, retailers or client to see. This sample is usually measured on a live model. The sample is used so the client can see how the garment works and fits and whether it needs any alterations to the design or manufacture to meet the client or retailer's needs.

Body scanning

Companies are now experimenting with using a computer and 3D virtual **modelling** techniques. This means that clients can see the product on screen instead of having a live model and can request modifications if necessary. The customer goes into a booth where a computer can map their body shape in as little as ten seconds. The body map can be used to make garments that fit the customer perfectly, as well as giving customers an impression of what a particular garment would look like on them without having to try it on. Customers could use this system of 'trying' garments at home using the Internet.

Production checks

Another way of checking or modifying the product is to make a sample using the specialized machinery in the sample room or on the production line. This will check that the whole manufacturing process is correct. A machinist will make a 'walk through' by going to each of the machines to be used and work through how the garment is made with the specialist operator. This will help ensure that the product can be made using the chosen method of production. Any modifications to the product can be made at this stage with the designer and the production manager.

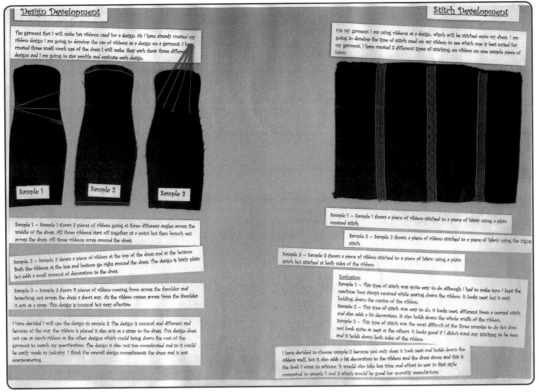

The student has made samples of her product, including stitching samples, and has evaluated each one

Quality control and assurance

Companies not only check that the product will be well made, but also that a sample (or pilot) production run of the product in the factory runs smoothly. This final check is to see that all the workers can make the product and that there are no other changes needed. They will make up all the sizes required to make sure that they conform to the product specifications. When everything is correctly in place, the **manufacturing specification** can be written.

These pilot runs provide information about the **quality control** measures that are needed to ensure that the product will be correctly made during production. Any mistakes made during final production would be costly in terms of material and time.

These checks will also form part of the company's **quality assurance**. This is the guarantee (assurance) to the customer that the product has been made to the highest possible standard from beginning to end. You will learn more about quality control and quality assurance in Chapters 7.3 and 7.4.

Coursework

You will need to produce a toile for your product. When that has been modified to correct any problems, you will be able to write your manufacturing specification. You must keep a record of your modifications and explain why you made them.

Test your knowledge

1 List three reasons for modifying a product.
2 Why does the designer need to refer to the specification when modifying the product?

Summary

★ Modifications are made to designs using samples to ensure that the final product is right for the market and for the production process.

Industrial processes and practices

Quality assurance

In this chapter you will:
★ **learn what quality assurance is**
★ **learn why it is important**
★ **learn to use evaluation and testing to check that a product is fit for purpose.**

Quality assurance

Quality assurance is a guarantee the manufacturer gives to the client or end-user. They guarantee that the product meets the following essential criteria:
- fitness for purpose
- correct price
- good technical performance of the product
- well thought out design or 'aesthetics' of the product
- that the statutory rights of the company and the consumer have been upheld; this ensures safe working practices and a safe end product
- that all codes of practice have been followed
- that the company has been externally assessed and achieved accreditation such as the BSI kitemark or CE mark (see Chapter 3.5).

Companies have developed 'Right first time every time', total quality management (TQM) or use the International Standard ISO 9000 (see Chapter 3.5) to help them create systems that ensure the products they make are fit for the market. TQM means that it is the responsibility of every member of the company to check that they understand what they are doing and that they do everything to the highest possible standard. So they check and keep checking the quality of each process. Quality checks will be included in the manufacturing specification and will be rigorously carried out to ensure the customer's needs and the required standards are consistently and economically met. This means that the company must have *trust* in their workforce, *focus* on the consumer, and actively *manage* the production of goods to ensure this.

These quality checks should cover:
- the design of the product
- the materials to be used, that is, the correct fabrics and components, and that they are of the correct standards

- the packaging of the product and the design of the packaging
- the correct product care and maintenance information
- customer service, answering any customer queries
- meeting customers' expectations.

The European safety standard (CE) mark

Feedback

For quality assurance to work well, all workers must know what they are checking for as the product goes through each stage of the design and manufacturing process. If there is a problem at any stage, feedback will inform the system so that it can be changed. At each checkpoint a decision is made. If the product meets the standard, it goes onto the next stage. If not, it goes back to be re-done and feedback is put into the production system to make any necessary adjustments. An example of a flow chart that includes quality checks and provides feedback can be seen on page 145.

Coursework

You will need to identify where feedback could be used to inform the making in your own work, and then show the modifications you have made as a result.

There are two main components of quality assurance: quality control and raw materials.

Quality control

Quality control comprises a range of tests that are carried out on all parts of the product throughout manufacturing. Quality control tests give vital feedback information about a product or its materials and components. These tests give clear guidance as to what is to be tested and what should happen if the product fails the test. You will learn more about quality control in Chapter 7.4.

Raw materials

The quality of the raw materials is important – you will not get a very high quality product from inferior materials. High quality materials will produce better results when adding finishes and interfacings and when testing the product for a reaction to heat. Testing at an early stage will also show how the product should be washed and cared for.

Planning and manufacture

A list of all the faults found during manufacture and making are recorded. This can mean, in the case of many faults occurring, that the product needs to be made differently. All aspects of the make-up of the product, such as the instructions for making and setting up correct sizes, need to be correct.

Final inspection

The finished garment or product is inspected to make sure it is the same as the production sample.

The use of ICT in quality assurance

Many companies will use **ICT** systems to help them keep a check on the product and its progress through the factory. They may use PDM (product data management) and EDP (electronic data processing) systems to analyse results and check product details.

Advantages of quality assurance

The advantages of having a quality assurance system in place are that:
- all documentation is available for inspection; this can help to protect a company from legal action if there is a problem
- all testing and instructions are listed, so everyone understands exactly what they are doing
- faulty goods are never sold
- a high quality specification is produced to ensure products are of consistent quality
- customers will feel more confident about buying the goods because they know they have been tested.

? Test your knowledge

1 Explain how TQM or quality assurance can ensure a high quality product.

2 Explain why trust is such an important part of TQM.

✎ Activities

Look at a soft toy and make a list of all the quality assurance checks needed to make it safe.

Summary

★ Quality assurance is a system that allows manufacturers to put in place practices and processes to help create a good product that is fit for purpose.

★ Quality assurance is applied to a product at all stages of its production, from design through to manufacture and being sold in shops.

Industrial processes and practices

Quality control

In this chapter you will:
★ learn what quality control is
★ learn the importance of quality control when designing and making textiles and fashion products
★ learn how to carry out quality control.

What is quality control?

Quality control is one aspect of the quality assurance system. Textiles products undergo key tests at every step of the manufacturing process to ensure they are of the required quality.

Companies have their own quality control departments, which use tests to make sure that all parts and components of a product are of the right quality, and that the product will be safe. Quality control checks help to prevent faults occurring. Companies will have in place a series of standard tests that make sure the quality is always high. From these they will set guidelines known as **tolerances**, which will state what is acceptable to the client and what is not. For example, the fabric must not shrink more than 0.1cm in 15 cm when washed.

Quality control tests

To make sure that products meet all the requirements, they need to be tested. This is done when the samples are made and the trial run of manufacturing is carried out. The tests may include checks to ensure that:
• each component is safe and fit for use
• the product conforms to the correct standards as laid down in legislation
• the size of the product is correct
• the tolerances are all being met
• the appearance and colour of the product matches the product specification
• the product is sufficiently durable
• the product meets the flammability regulations
• the final product is fit for purpose.

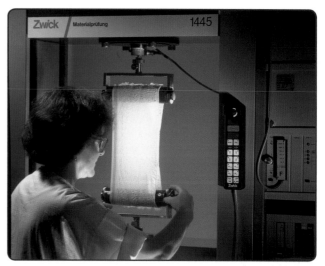

Testing seam tolerance

Tests are carried out to test specific aspects of a product, such as the effect of perspiration or whether pilling occurs (bobbles on the surface of fabric). Tests will also ensure that the dye does not run when the fabric is washed.

Specification sheets

The design and production teams will then use the results of these tests to modify the product, where necessary, and then create specification sheets to summarize all the information about the product. These are similar to your product and manufacturing specifications. They need to be clearly laid out and show all the points relating to quality control in the manufacturing process. Clear diagrams will be included showing all views of the product.

Feedback

Quality control is an important part of the manufacturing process. Manufacturers will look at each stage in the production to see what risks could occur and how they can be controlled or prevented. Feeding back the results of quality control helps to ensure that the faults can be located and systems put in place to solve the problem.

The table below gives an example of how manufacturers look at the potential risks in all stages of the production process and create feedback to put the faults right.

Testing samples

When making one-off products, the accepted tolerances may be different to those used when making a product in large numbers. It is easy to test a one-off product, but when hundreds or thousands of products are being made, the manufacturers can only really test a certain number of products. Therefore the manufacturer will set a limit on the number of products being spot-checked; this is called a sample. The results of testing the sample will let the company know whether they need to do further tests or change the way in which a product is being made, or let production continue.

Many manufacturers use **CAD** and **CAM** to help them with their quality control testing. They employ ICT experts to write special programmes that will automatically check things such as machine settings. However, not everything can be checked in this way.

Coursework

You should set up your own system for checking your product and then putting feedback into the way you make the product.

Activity

Look at a child's soft toy and then make a chart like the one below which lists all the quality control checks that would be needed to make it.

Summary

★ Quality control is a key part of the production process and should be carried out at each stage of making.

★ Feedback from testing allows the product to be modified and improved in order to meet the product specification.

Production system step	Risk	Reason why it is a risk	Control/feedback
Cutting fabric	Cut to wrong size	Pieces will not fit together	Make a toile to check fit and feedback the information Use CAM to help ensure accuracy of cutting
Joining the seams using a sewing machine	The seam allowance used is too large or small	If the seam allowance is too large, the end product will be too small. If it is too small, the end product will be too large	Use a seam guide to keep it the correct width
	There are missed stitches	The wrong type or size of machine needle is being used, or the needle is not sharp. The product will not be securely joined	Check the type, size and sharpness of the needle, feedback the information on needle type and when the needle was last replaced, and replace if necessary
Pressing the end product	There are watermarks	The iron setting is not high enough to produce steam	See if the fabric can be pressed at a high enough temperature for steam. If not, use a dry iron

An example of a risk assessment for the production of a shirt

Industrial processes and practices

Care labelling

In this chapter you will:
★ **learn about the information given on the labels of all textiles products.**

In 1986, the Textiles Products Regulations were introduced to make it compulsory to show the fibre content of all textiles products. This followed the earlier legislation of 1976, which made it compulsory to label textiles products. Failure to label could lead to a manufacturer being prosecuted; equally, failure to follow the instructions given may lead to a loss of consumer rights.

The labelling scheme ensures:
• that information about the fibre content and the care needed to maintain the quality of the product is provided to the customer
• that the manufacturer is conforming to European Union (EU) standards; labelling methods and the names of fibres are kept the same (standardized) throughout the EU
• that stock control is enhanced; sometimes labels have barcodes printed on them to help the retailer control their stock.

Labelling is compulsory for all products that have more than 80 per cent textile content and are unused.

Care labels may be sewn into a garment at the back of the neck, into a side seam or onto the waistband. They may also be glued in the case of small items such as gloves.

These are permanent labels. Care labelling may also be found on a swing tag attached to the garment or stuck to the packaging.

Label information

Care labels should carry the following information:
• fibre content
• garment size
• washing instructions
• drying instructions, such as do not tumble dry or dry flat
• warnings, for example whether the product is fragile or may leak dye on first wash, as in 'wash dark colours separately'
• dry cleaning information
• ironing instructions.

Care labels may also state the country of manufacture and they may carry a manufacturer's address. Care label information may be shown as symbols, like the ones illustrated opposite. Care should be taken to read and understand the labels, as ignoring the information given could affect your consumer rights.

Smart labelling

In industry, the PAXAR 676 high-resolution printer uses CAM to print care labels onto a range of satin, polyester and nylon fabrics. The labels are then cut and stacked automatically using **ultrasonic cutters** and stacker units. These machines can read the label and cut it in the right place. This greatly reduces the costs of producing labels. The ultrasonic cutter gives a smooth soft edge to the label to avoid irritation to the user.

〔40°〕	MACHINE: WARM MINIMUM WASH 40°C	HANDWASH: WARM 40°C DO NOT RUB
WASH DARK COLOURS SEPARATELY. WASH INSIDE OUT. RINSE THOROUGHLY. SHORT SPIN. DO NOT WRING. AVOID DIRECT HEAT AND SUNLIGHT. WASH USING A WOOLMARK APPROVED DETERGENT		

DO NOT BLEACH	WARM IRON	DRY CLEANABLE	TUMBLE DRYABLE

0049

Information on a care label

The Paxar 676 high-resolution printer

Washing

Symbol	Meaning
[40]	Maximum temperature 40°C Mechanical action normal Rinsing and spinning normal
[40]	Maximum temperature 40°C Mechanical action reduced Rinse with gradual cooling Spinning reduced
[40]	Maximum temperature 40°C Mechanical action much reduced Rinsing/spinning normal
[hand]	Hand wash only

Washing continued

Symbol	Meaning
[tub crossed]	Do not wash
[triangle Cl]	Chlorine bleach can be used
[triangle crossed]	Do not bleach

Drying

Symbol	Meaning
[circle in square]	Tumble drying beneficial
[square crossed]	Do not tumble dry
[|||]	Drip dry, soaking wet
[–]	Dry flat
[hang]	Hang to dry

Ironing

Symbol	Meaning
[iron 1 dot]	Cool iron
[iron 2 dots]	Warm iron
[iron 3 dots]	Hot iron
[iron crossed]	Do not iron

Dry cleaning

Symbol	Meaning
(A)	Dry clean in all solvents
(P)	Dry clean in perchloroethylene
(F)	Dry clean in certain solvents only
[circle crossed]	Do not dry clean

Symbols on care labels and their meanings

Coursework

You should produce a care label for your product. You will need to consider all the points normally found on a care label. You might enhance your ICT marks by printing the information directly onto the label fabric.

Activity

Use the list of label information above to help you design and make a label for your textile product.

Summary

★ Labelling is essential for the correct care and maintenance of textiles products.

★ In industry, labels can be applied quickly and efficiently using CAM.

Industrial processes and practices

Patterns

In this chapter you will:
★ **learn about basic blocks**
★ **learn how to use patterns to control quality**
★ **learn how to use a commercial pattern.**

Designers and manufacturers need to take designs and turn these into finished products. This is done using patterns.

What is a pattern?

A **pattern** is a 2D template that is used to make a 3D product. This template is called a pattern piece, or in industry it is referred to as a marker or block.

The pattern is made from paper or card and is made up of individual pieces, which when put together form the whole product. The pattern pieces are placed on fabric, which is then cut out and sewn together to make the product. Allowance will have to be made for seams to be joined (the seam allowance is taken as 1.5 cm unless otherwise stated) and for shaping.

Patterns can be drafted (drawn) by hand or by computer.

Quality control

Creating patterns is an essential part of the design and product development process, and it is important that the pattern is correct before manufacturing begins. When textiles products are made on a large scale, each and every one must be the same, and a pattern helps to ensure this. This is part of quality control. A sample pattern is made and then checked to make sure the product made from it will be of the right quality. The pattern can then be modified before production begins.

Basic blocks

A **basic block** is the starting point for producing a pattern for clothing. They are 2D shapes, produced from a detailed set of measurements, for each section of a garment. In the example of a skirt, the minimum number of pieces would be a front, back and waistband, although there could be more, such as a pocket.

When made up, the basic blocks would form a basic garment with no special style features, like pockets or pleats. This block pattern then needs to be adapted to form different styles. The block is cut from card so it can be reused, and it has no seam allowances – these are added to the pattern later, together with the style details.

Basic blocks are made in sizes that conform to the British Standards Institute (BSI) **standard sizing** and are produced from regular surveys of average measurements. The last survey was carried out between 2002–3. Clothing manufacturers use these standard sizes as their clothes have to fit many different people.

Size 10 SBS 3666U	Bust 82–6 cm Waist 66–70 cm Hip 90–4 cm
Size 12 SBS 3666U	Bust 86–90 cm Waist 70–4 cm Hip 94–8 cm
Size 14 SBS 3666U	Bust 92–4 cm Waist 74–8 cm Hip 98–102 cm
Size 16 SBS 3666U	Bust 94–8 cm Waist 78–82 cm Hip 102–106 cm

BSI standard dress sizes

In industry, a **pattern technician** (a person with a very good knowledge of both design and construction) will convert the basic block into a pattern for a given design.

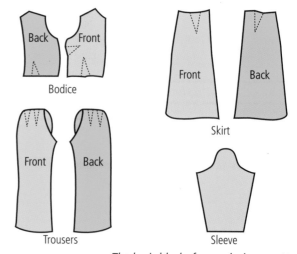

The basic blocks for producing a pattern

Commercial patterns

- Fabric shops and department stores carry large books of patterns from different manufacturers for home dressmakers to choose from.
- These patterns are produced from basic blocks and are adapted to a particular style. They are made from fine tissue paper and need to be handled with care.
- The patterns are very carefully tested by the manufacturer to make sure that they work and the instructions are easily understood.
- Before you start to use a pattern, you should read all the instructions carefully.

Pattern information

Each pattern carries an explanation of the pattern markings, a list of the pattern pieces, sample layouts for the pattern and detailed instructions for making it. On the outside of the envelope there will be front and back views of the product (see Chapter 7.8), a list of suggested fabrics and components (notions) as well as the quantity of fabric required for each size.

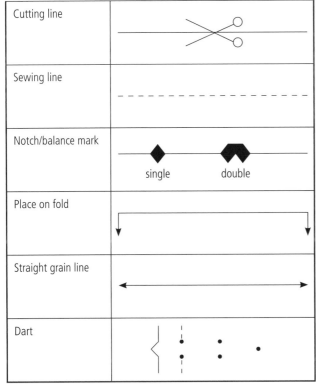

Cutting line	
Sewing line	
Notch/balance mark	single double
Place on fold	
Straight grain line	
Dart	

Symbols on patterns

Pattern sizing

It is important to remember that patterns work on average sizes, and adjustments may be needed for a perfect fit. Some patterns are sold as multi-size, which means that they have several sizes printed on each piece. This can be very helpful when trying to get a perfect fit.

Ease

Patterns are produced to body measurements, with an allowance for movement and function. This allowance will vary. For example, a winter jacket is designed to fit over other clothes but a summer dress will have little under it. This allowance is called the 'ease'.

All of this work in designing patterns used to be done by hand, and still is for bespoke or tailoring work.

Activity

Working as a group, disassemble a garment to find the pattern pieces used. Work out the seam allowance and the ease on the garment. Keep the pattern pieces to use for the activity in the next chapter.

Summary

★ Basic blocks are the starting point for all patterns and can be adapted to suit any style requirements.

★ Patterns are a useful part of quality control.

Using CAD and CAM to plan patterns

7.7

In this chapter you will:

★ **learn to use CAD and CAM to produce a pattern**

★ **learn about lay planning.**

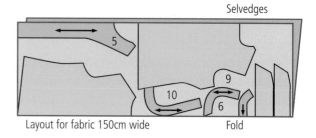

Layout for fabric 150cm wide   Fold

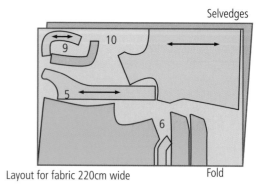

Layout for fabric 220cm wide   Fold

The use of CAD

The use of CAD and ICT has simplified the process of creating patterns by using an electronic tape measure or a 3D body scanner to get precise measurements. The military use this type of system to create bespoke garments, such as dress uniforms, that must fit perfectly.

Measurements can be inserted into a computerized measuring system, which creates a database of measurements. These can be referred to when designing products. Creating size charts and sized patterns for a product enables designers to produce a pattern with different fits such as loose fit, standard fit and close fit, and with different sizes. By using pattern software to develop, adapt and print the pattern block, the manufacturer and the client are also able to see the how the end product will work in 3D.

Lay planning

Once the pattern has been made, a cutting layout or **lay plan** is produced. This means arranging the pattern pieces on the fabric, usually by hand, to ensure the best use of the material. The pattern pieces are moved around to see how they fit best within the fabric, before being cut out. On commercial patterns, instructions are included to show how the pattern pieces can be laid out on different widths of fabric. The pieces will need to be laid out differently, depending on the width of the fabric, to allow you to use the fabric economically; look at the example opposite. Laying out pattern pieces by hand would not be suitable for large-scale production.

The lay plan will also have to take account of any directional pattern on the fabric so that all the pieces are cut the same way. If the pattern has figures printed on it, they must all be the right way up when the product is assembled. The lay plan must also allow for a pile or

napped fabric, such as velvet or corduroy, to be cut in the same direction, otherwise the light will reflect differently from the different pieces giving a light and dark effect. In both of these cases, extra fabric will be needed.

Lay planning in industry

In industry, the use of ICT means that lay planning can be done more quickly and more accurately using a computer. The pattern pieces are laid out to minimize the wastage of material and therefore reduce costs. From this, manufacturers can work out how much fabric is needed and the amount of waste; this is called **efficiency**. The machine operator has to consider the characteristics of the material, as different materials react differently to cutting. Information about the width of the fabric is also considered and the computer programme can work out the efficient lay of the fabric, with the aid of the lay planner.

Using computerized equipment means that the pieces can be moved around on screen to get the best fit; often there are several ways of arranging pattern pieces. Pattern pieces for several different products or different sizes of the same product can be laid onto one piece of fabric at the same time.

If you were making a single product, you would fold the fabric and lay out the pattern pieces on the folded fabric.

direction and can be matched. The pieces are then cut out by a computer-controlled device that uses either laser or mechanical cutters. These ensure that all pattern pieces are of the correct size and are accurate.

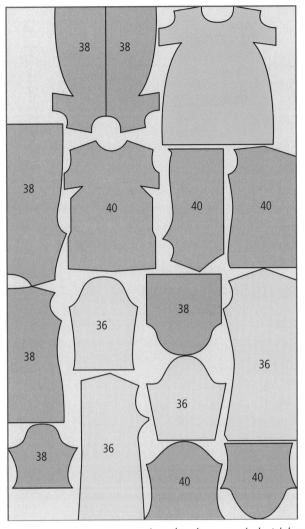

Lay planning on an industrial scale

A laser cutter

Activity

Use the pattern pieces from your disassembly activity in Chapter 7.6 and work out a lay plan for 150 cm wide fabric and for 90 cm wide fabric. How much fabric would you need for each of these?

This would mean that both sides of the garment could be cut out at once. However, in industry, pieces are always laid on a flat piece of fabric and pattern pieces are created for front and back, and left and right. Using CAD and CAM means that pieces can be cut very accurately and less fabric is wasted.

Summary

★ The use of computers has changed the way in which patterns are developed and laid out. This is now faster, more accurate, and less waste fabric is produced.

Cutting

The lay plan information is sent to a laser cutter and the fabric is spread out by a computerized spreader, which can spread up to ten layers of fabric at a time quickly and faultlessly. The spreader can be programmed with information as to how the fabric should be laid out in order to avoid wastage so that patterns will run in the same

Industrial processes and practices

In this chapter you will:
★ learn about using commercial patterns.

Commercial patterns

Commercial patterns can be selected from the large catalogues of patterns held in fabric stores. There are hundreds of patterns in each catalogue and they are available in a wide range of sizes. Mostly these patterns are kept in the store, but if not they can be ordered.

Each pattern will give different views of the product, showing how it could be changed for different needs, such as different collars, lengths or sleeve types. It will also show the front and back views of each option.

The pattern envelope contains all the information needed to buy the fabric and the components (referred to as notions on the pattern). The 'yardage', how much material is required, is given in both metric and imperial measurements, and is shown for each view on the envelope. It is also shown for the most common widths of fabric available. There are also suggestions for the type of fabric and components that would be suitable and advice against those that would be unsuitable. For example, diagonal stripes would not be suitable for a design that has many very small pieces, as it would be too difficult to match them all up.

Inside the pattern envelope are the pattern pieces for all the views; these are made of tissue paper and need to be handled with care. The enclosed instruction sheet will tell you which pattern pieces you need for each view, how to lay them out on the fabric (options are given for different fabric widths) and how to make up the product.

Remember, you need to read the pattern envelope before buying fabric and the instruction sheet before starting work.

The paper pattern

A pattern piece is supplied for each piece of the product on the pattern, and printed on each piece is all the information needed for placing it on the fabric and cutting out.

The pieces also carry markings to show the placement of pockets, darts and other features. All of these markings need to be transferred to the cut fabric with either tailor's tacks or by using a tracing wheel and tailor's carbon paper.

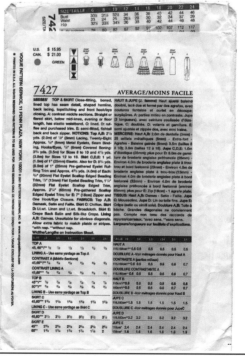

The front and back of a commercial pattern

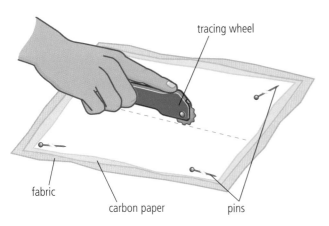

Transferring markings using carbon paper

If using carbon paper, it must be tailor's carbon paper as this will always wash out of the fabric.

Some patterns are made so that the measurements for several sizes are printed on each piece. This can be confusing, so it is important to follow the instructions very carefully in order to get the correct sizing. If four seams were all cut on the wrong cutting line, the error in the finished product would be eight times the size of the original error! This is because each seam is made up of two pieces of fabric. However, printing multiple sizes like this reduces costs for the pattern manufacturer, and therefore for the consumer.

Making your own patterns

If you choose to make your own patterns, you will need a basic pattern block that can be made to fit you exactly. While the fit is personalized for you, nevertheless it is a complex task and you may not be able to fit this into your available time. A way round this could be to use a software package that will allow you to input your measurements, design your garment and then print out the pattern. These are excellent, but if the pattern is printed on A4 paper, it can be fiddly piecing it together. You can also make your own patterns using specialized computer drafting programmes such as Propattern, Fittingly sew or Wild things. These programmes display the pattern on a computer screen and allow the pattern to be adapted by either changing the measurements or changing the size of the pattern on screen.

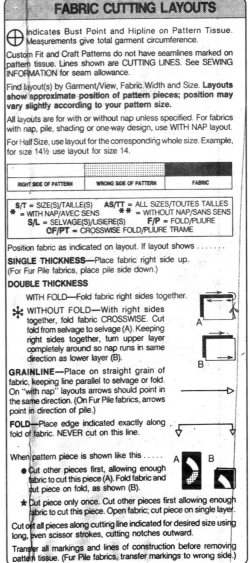

Some markings from a commercial pattern

Activity

Take the pattern pieces from a paper pattern and lay them out as shown in the pattern layout. Work out how much fabric you will need to make a garment for yourself.

Summary

★ It is easier to use a commercial pattern than to make one.

★ You need to follow the instructions carefully and transfer all the pattern markings.

Industrial processes and practices

In this chapter you will:

★ **learn the role that costing plays in the development of a new product**

★ **learn how to cost your product.**

Costing is an essential part of any product development, and the overall cost boundaries will have been set very early in the designing process as part of the design specification. A constant check will be kept on the cost of the product throughout the development process.

More new product ideas are left undeveloped for costing reasons than for any other reason. In order for a product to be successful, it must be cost effective so that it will be purchased and the designer, manufacturer and retailer can make a profit. Each additional stage in manufacture incurs extra making and checking costs.

Conformance and non-conformance

It is also essential to ensure that the end product is of the highest quality, as faulty products cost money. The extra costs in faulty goods arise because the goods may have to be replaced, because of a loss of confidence from the client who may go elsewhere in future, and possibly even through fines if the faulty product causes actual damage or harm to the client. These are referred to as:

- costs of **conformance**: the cost of producing high quality goods with very few faults
- costs of **non-conformance**: the additional costs incurred by faulty goods and the need for extra quality inspections, testing and the consequent reduced price of substandard goods.

Direct and indirect costs

In industry, costing must include every aspect of making the product, so not only the **direct** costs of materials, components and labour to make the product but also the **indirect** or 'hidden' costs of:

- research
- designing
- testing
- equipment
- utilities such as electricity used to power the machines
- storage of materials
- training
- quality checks
- packaging
- advertising
- delivery
- profit for the manufacturing company
- profit at the point of sale.

Retailers purchase the product from the manufacturer and then increase the price to make their own profit. In some cases, this mark up at the point of sale may be well in excess of 100 per cent of the **wholesale price** (the price that the retailer buys at). For example, a bespoke christening outfit, consisting of christening robe, petticoat and bonnet, made exclusively for a high street store might cost £45 for the materials and £100 to be made. It might go on sale for a total of £310 with each part being sold separately. The extra £165 goes towards paying for the retailer's premises, the actual building maintenance costs as well as the decor, the rates or taxes on the building, the staff wages and the profit.

BREAKDOWN OF SELLING PRICE	
Cost of marketing	30%
Labour	5%
Packaging	5%
Overheads	20%
Marketing	10%
Retailer's cost and profit	30%

Breakdown of the selling price of a bespoke Christening outfit

Costing your product

The design specification for your coursework should include a budget guideline, which you will need to consider carefully at all times. Your budget will include the costs of:

- materials: it is sensible when purchasing fabric to allow a little extra in the event of mistakes

COSTING SHEET

Costing Chart

Item	Quantity	Cost	Total x1	Total x10	Total x100	Total x1000
Silver Shantung	0.6	£8.95	5.37	53.7	537	5370
Grey Whisper Taffeta Lining	0.6	£3.95	2.37	23.7	237	2370
25cm Grey Zip	1	£1.69	1.69	16.9	169	1690
Boning	0.8	£0.50	0.4	4	40	400
Pale grey sewing thread	1	£0.99	0.99	9.9	99	990
Packet of pale blue beads	1	£0.90	0.9	9	90	900
Packet of silver beads	1	£0.90	0.9	9	90	900
Packet of silver sequins	1	£1.25	1.25	12.5	125	1250
Embroidery thread silver	1	£1.90	1.9	19	190	1900
Embroidery thread white	1	£1.75	1.75	17.5	175	1750
Interfacing	0.6	£2.40	1.44	14.4	144	1440
			17.52	175.2	1752	17520

Why the cost of materials only represents 30% of the selling price.

When a factory decides how much to charge for a textiles product the materials only count towards 30% of the final cost. There are the costs of many other things such as design prototypes, labour costs, running of the factory, administration charges, packaging and distribution. The final selling price of the product also has to include the costs of marketing, advertising and the retailer's cost and profit margin. In industry computer costing systems are used so accurate product costs are made because these are essential for good business management. The chart is one way to breakdown the final cost and it can be used to find out the final selling price. However there are factors that can effect the price of textiles products, it depends where the product is sold, the name of the designer and the price that customers are prepared to pay for the product. There are also ways to the reduce the price by buying things in bulk, by buying cheaper alternatives but still of good quality and there other methods to reduce the price of textile products.

Breakdown of selling price

Jenny Ridgewell supplied this breakdown of selling price.

Cost of materials- 30%
Labour- 5%
Packaging- 5%
Overheads and profit- 20%
Marketing and advertising- 10%
Retailer's cost and profit- 30%

The breakdown of my selling price for my product

This is the breakdown of the selling price if the product was mass produced commercially and sold.

Cost of materials- £17.52
Labour- £2.92
Packaging- £2.92
Overheads and profit- £11.68
Marketing and advertising- £5.48
Retailer's cost and profit- £17.52
Total- £58.04

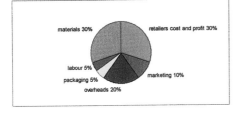

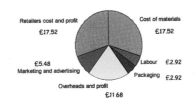

A student's costing sheet showing the breakdown of the selling price

- components
- the pattern if you are not making your own.

You should present the data in a spreadsheet similar to the one shown in the illustration; this not only gives the details needed but also adds to your ICT marks for the use of the spreadsheet and to your marks for industrial processes. You could improve the information given by adding columns showing how the costs multiply for more than one product, but you need to remember that, in industry, costs for materials can be reduced by buying in bulk. You can use the information on the back of a commercial pattern to help you estimate the cost of making a product.

You should evaluate your final costs and say if you consider the product to be value for money. You could also indicate where costs could be reduced by multiple production or through the use of CAD/CAM. You also need to refer back to your initial budget and say if you have managed to keep to it and, if not, why not. What has caused it to go up or down?

✏ Activities

1. Draw up a spreadsheet to cost out your final product. Make a list to help you do this so that you do not forget anything.

2. Now make a list of the additional costs that might be incurred if this product was manufactured in industry.

Summary

★ Accurate costing is an important factor in designing and making products and there are many hidden features to consider.

★ In some cases, it may actually be cheaper to produce high quality goods because of the cost of conformance.

Industrial processes and practices

7.10 Planning a production system

> **In this chapter you will:**
> ★ learn about planning a production system.

When manufacturing textiles products, it is important to ensure that the product is designed, made and delivered on time. When planning the production, you must decide what tasks need to be done, in what order, and for how long, in order to ensure this. You also need to build in time for **evaluation** and quality control checks of each step. A **work schedule** or plan of the work to be done is very important when you are planning for large volume production. Any mistake in the plan could result in production coming to a halt or being delayed, costing the company time and money.

The GANTT chart

Once you know the **time span** of the project, you need to draw up a schedule showing how long will be devoted to each task, what order the tasks will be completed in and whether any of the tasks will overlap with each other. This is called a **GANTT chart** and can be produced using spreadsheet software. The GANTT chart lists all the processes involved in producing the product and shows the time allocated to each process. This will show you whether any processes will overlap and whether your production process will fit in the time allowed.

Flow chart/system diagram

You should also make a **flow chart** or **system diagram** showing where decisions are made, quality control checks are carried out and how the feedback re-informs the system. Look at this example opposite.

This system will include all the information that is gathered for the manufacturing specification (see Chapter 7.11).

HOURS	1	2	3	4	5	6	7	8	9	10	11	12	13	14	15
Make a paper template	■														
Cut the fabric for a toile	■														
Insert a zip fastener between the two halves of the back		■	■	■											
Open the zip					■										
Tack and machine the edge							■								
Turn to the right side									■						
Press										■					
Evaluate toile											■				
Modify if necessary												■	■	■	■
Adjust the pattern if necessary															
Cut the fabric for the cushion															
Size check															
Insert zip fastener in the back															
Quality check															
Open the zip															
Tack and then sew the edge seams															
Check seams															
Turn to the right side															
Press															
Final check															

A Gantt chart

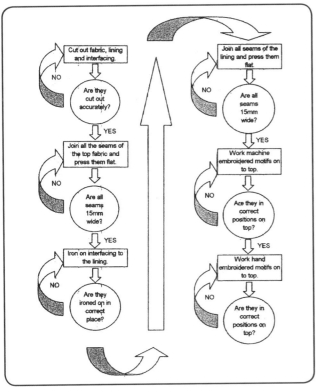

An example flowchart/system diagram

Planning in the fashion and textiles industry

For each product that is made, a plan is created to show how long it takes to make the product. A sample machinist will make the product to check that all the pieces fit together. In order to make sure that the product works on the factory floor, a mini production simulation is set up and each stage is timed. The information gathered will enable the production team to know if the machine operators can make the product. It will identify any problem areas or things that may need to be changed, and indicate how long each task will take. From this, an accurate work schedule can be drawn up, which may include accurate diagrams of the processes to be carried out. The work schedule, the diagrams and the time plan can be set up using specialist CAD programmes. This helps ensure accuracy and saves time.

Product production

The production of a product can be divided into three stages.

- Stage 1: sub-assembly – this might include joining and attaching small components, or attaching labels.
- Stage 2: final assembly – this will include joining major parts of the product together.
- Stage 3: finishing – this includes the final pressing of the product to maximize its presentation.

At the end of the process, there is an inspection to check the final product for any defects. (You often find small stickers inside garments with a number on them; these are the checkers' numbers.) Finally, the product is folded and/or packed.

Ic Coursework

As you will be working within a tight time frame, it is a good idea to plan your time allocation by using a GANTT chart to plot your activities.

Activity

Draw up a system for making a cushion using tie dyed fabric.

Summary

★ Planning is an important part of the design and production process and you must be able to produce and work to detailed working schedules.

★ You must also be able to set and work to realistic deadlines for all stages of designing and making.

Industrial processes and practices

7.11 Manufacturing specifications

In this chapter you will:

★ learn what makes a good manufacturing specification.

The manufacturing specification

A manufacturing or final product specification is a detailed specification written once the final product has been developed. It explains exactly what the product is and how it will be made. It can be a mixture of statements, drawings and flow charts. A manufacturing specification should provide enough information about the product so that anyone could use the specification to make the same product again and again.

A manufacturing specification is used by manufacturing companies to ensure that a product will always be made in the same way, with the same equipment, and to the same quality, wherever it is made. The manufacturing specification may repeat some of the information given in the product specification and should include the following details.

- The fabric used: quality, quantity, colour, cost.
- The components used: quality, quantity, colour, cost.
- The tools and equipment to be used at each stage in the making, with information about the changes needed for mass production.
- The process of making in simple steps.
- Tolerances allowed in the making; for example a seam must be 1.5 cm wide +/– 0.1 cm.
- The time to be spent on each process.
- Health and safety considerations.

For complex products, this will be a very long document and may take a company a long time to complete. The manufacturing specification can be used to produce a one-off product, a batch of products or to mass-produce the product. If it is to be used for mass production, the equipment used will need to be changed. For example, you may use scissors to cut out the pieces for a one-off product but a laser cutter would be used to cut out 2000 products.

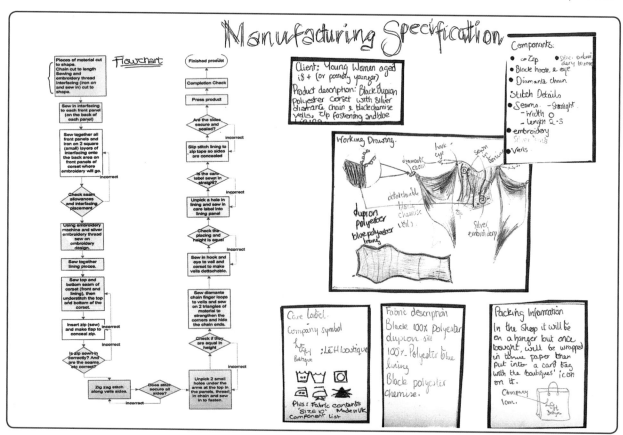

A student's manufacturing specification for a corset

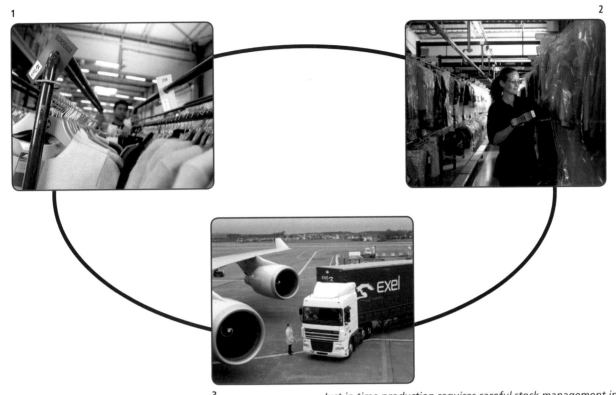

3

Just in time production requires careful stock management in order to avoid delays in production and distribution

Prototypes

It is important that all the information needed to manufacture the product is laid out clearly and is easy to understand. This care should extend to any samples or prototypes that have been made to test the manufacturing process. The prototype must be accurate and precise for the manufacturing specification to work, as all the information needed is tested out when the prototype is made.

Just in time (JIT)

If a manufacturing specification is to work, all the materials must be readily available for the work to be done, otherwise there will be expensive hold-ups in the manufacturing process. Most manufacturers now use the just in time (JIT) system to help ensure this. JIT is a computer-based system that lets companies track stocks of materials and components to ensure that they all arrive at the factory just when they are needed. This is stock control. It means that the company does not have to store large quantities of stock nor spend too much money in advance. One of the disadvantages of the JIT system, however, is that there can be no mistakes or there will be a delay in production.

Coursework

You need to write a manufacturing specification for your final product

Test your knowledge

1 Using the information in this chapter to help you, write a manufacturing specification for a drawstring bag made from two pieces of fabric. You need to specify the fabric used.

Summary

★ In order for manufacture to run smoothly and produce consistent quality products, there needs to be a detailed manufacturing specification for workers to follow. In addition, all the materials and components must be available.

Industrial processes and practices

Industrial processes

> **In this chapter you will:**
> ★ learn about CAM
> ★ learn why CAM is used in industry.

Computer aided manufacture (CAM)

CAM stands for computer aided manufacture and refers to computers used to control machinery when producing textiles products. Computer aided manufacture includes a wide range of activities that are carried out with the use of computer-controlled equipment, from printers, computerized sewing and knitting machines, through to plotters and laser cutters.

The benefits of using CAM are that it:
- saves time, labour and costs in industry
- provides consistency and accuracy in the finished product
- helps to provide a safer workplace by having built-in controls that can stop the machine if it malfunctions. For example, a laser cutter only works within a given area and cannot cut outside that area.

Many CAM machines are linked directly to CAD programmes so designs can be transferred straight from CAD to the machine that will make all or part of the finished product.

Uses of CAM in industry

Weaving looms

Designs can be sent to the weaving loom and then woven using computer-controlled looms. Colours can be changed as well as the weave.

Knitting machines

Garment designs and styles can be sent to a knitting machine and then individual pieces can be knitted or whole garments can be knitted without seams. This is called 3D knitting technology or whole garment technology.

Embroidery machines

Designs are sent to special machines that can embroider motifs, logos, words (referred to as monograms) or patterns accurately and quickly.

Printing

Transferring images onto fabrics using digital printing is used in different ways and for different reasons depending on the fabric, the cost and the needs of the client. Sometimes it is used to produce sample print lengths. This reduces costs as it means that you can check the design and colour of small samples. These samples could then

3D knitting technology

A computerised embroidery machine

be used to make up a sample product to test whether the design should be used.

Once the design has been created or modified on the computer, it can then be sent to the printer to print the design onto the fabric.

Lay plans and cutting out

A pattern layout can be designed using CAD and then sent to the CAM machines. The information is sent to the plotter, to be adjusted if need be for the specific fabric, and then to the spreader, which will lay the fabric out quickly and accurately. The laser cutter then cuts out the fabric. This means that many layers of cloth can be cut at once, a lot quicker that one person cutting out.

Sewing machines

Machines can be adapted for sewing repetitive or long tasks, such as trouser seams. Machines can also be programmed, depending on the product that is being made, so that information such as the stitch length or the seam width can be put in and changed for each item. You will also find computer-controlled sewing machines used for specialized tasks such as darts and pleats, attaching waistbands, attaching buttonholes, or attaching pockets.

Coursework

Most of the CAM equipment used in industry will not be available in school. However, you may have a computerized sewing, knitting or embroidery machine. You may also be able to use a printer to transfer print or print directly onto fabric. Where possible, you should consider using CAM to improve the accuracy and efficiency of making your product.

Test your knowledge

1 Why would it be more economical to produce a machine knitted product rather than a hand knitted one?

2 Why would a haute couture garment be more likely to have hand embroidery and beading than a prêt-á-porter product?

Summary

★ CAM is used to save time and energy while providing a consistent and accurate product.

★ It can be used both in mass production and in the production of individual products.

★ Digital printing and imaging on textiles are part of this process.

Advertising and marketing

In this chapter you will:
★ learn about advertising
★ learn about marketing
★ learn about packaging as a marketing tool.

In order to sell products to consumers, textiles and fashion products need to be marketed and advertised.

Marketing

Marketing is a method of promoting products to customers. It involves creating a plan to ensure that the product reaches the right end-user, or what is called the 'market segment'. It includes market research and sometimes product development, as well as informing customers about products.

The marketing of a product is linked closely to trends and lifestyles. The marketing department will look for the interests of the target group in order to find the most appropriate means of marketing a product. For example, if they are marketing a product for very young children, they may advertise it through mother and child magazines.

Advertising

Advertising is any form of media which informs and influences existing or new customers. Companies use advertising as a means of letting customers know about a product. Background research into the product and the market will be collected by specialist agencies, or a company's in-house design team, who will create a range of advertising material to promote the product. Advertising a product is very expensive and many companies will ensure that this aspect is costed as part of the development of a new product. The final cost of the product includes all the expenses incurred in arriving at and making the product.

Advertising can be used to:
• inform consumers of new products or product launches
• influence customers about which products to buy
• keep existing customers loyal to the product
• show all consumers how the product will suit their needs.

Methods of advertising

Companies will use different methods of advertising to reach a wide audience:
• the media: for example, television, radio and cinema
• magazines and newspapers for the public as well as trade publications
• leaflets, posters, advertisements and fliers
• websites and Internet pop-ups.

More and more companies are now using the Internet in order to reach more people to market their textiles products. Using this method also means that information can be quickly updated.

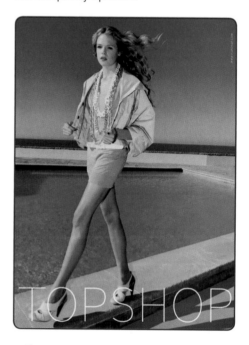

Advertising in magazines

Different methods of advertising are used to appeal to different groups. For example, a product for young men might be advertised on popular websites or magazines targeted at that age group.

Protection for the consumer

There are regulations in place that tell companies what they can and cannot put into advertisements; these regulations also protect the consumer. All advertising is controlled by a body called the Advertising Standards Authority (ASA). The ASA have a strict code of practice, which ensures that adverts do not mislead the consumer or make false claims.

Other bodies, such as the Trading Standards Service, also regulate how companies advertise and describe their products. They inform the consumer about their rights should the product they purchase be faulty.

Companies can use advertising to recall products after they have gone on sale. This may happen because a fault has only been noticed after the product has been put on sale.

Display

The ways in which products are displayed affects how well they will sell. For example, in shops and stores, information about new products can be found at the point of sale (the cash desk) and in eye-catching positions in the windows and near doors. Items might be grouped by style or by colour. Whole outfits or whole room settings are displayed to show how items can look and to encourage customers to look at a whole range of items.

Designers use fashion shows to display their brand new or exclusive collections prior to each season. Retailers use these to find new stock ideas for their outlets. Catalogues also provide a useful means of shopping from home, which is particularly helpful for customers who may find visiting shops difficult.

Packaging

Many goods that are purchased are packaged. Products are packaged to protect the goods, provide product information or promote the product.

Many textiles products do not need packaging; most garments are not packaged so that they can be tried on. However, items that are considered fragile, such as lacy garments, may be covered or protected.

Information on the packaging must not only alert the customer to any risks associated with the packaging, such as the danger polythene bags pose to young children, but also give details of how to safely dispose of the packaging. The packaging should also state if it is recyclable or biodegradable and should not have too many unwanted layers. Companies have a responsibility to consider the environment when selecting their packaging.

Firms may advertise related products on the packaging of a product and also on the swing tags. Swing tags also give details of price and sizing.

Swing tags can be used to advertise related products

Coursework

Although you should consider the packaging of your textiles product, you do not need to actually design or make the packaging.

Test your knowledge

1 Why are the ASA and Trading Standards Service important to the consumer when buying goods?

2 List three reasons why companies advertise products.

Activity

Find three items that have been advertised in different ways and explain why you think each method was chosen and what it might have achieved.

Summary

★ Advertising and marketing are vital in promoting new or updated products to new or existing clients.

★ Advertising and marketing are carefully regulated to protect the consumer.

★ Packaging plays an important part in both advertising and marketing, and companies have a responsibility to protect the environment in their choice of packaging.

Industrial processes and practices

Exam questions

1 Products must be made to a very high standard or they will not sell. The quality department set tolerance levels for products. What do tolerance levels mean?

(2 marks)

2 What is meant by batch production? *(2 marks)*

3 Cost is important. List three ways in which a manufacturer can cut the cost of making products.

(3 marks)

4 Modern factories use computerised sewing machines when manufacturing products.

Explain the advantages of using computerised sewing machines. *(4 marks)*

5 Pattern laying is an important process in the manufacturing industry. Discuss the ways in which computer technology helps at this stage of manufacture.

(4 marks)

6 A manufacturing specification is needed for your product. List four things that need to be included on a manufacturing specification. *(4 marks)*

(AQA 2003)

8 Doing your coursework project

Coursework accounts for 60 per cent of your total marks for the course. You should spend no longer than 40 hours on your coursework for the full course, or 20 hours for the short course. Although this sounds like a great many hours, in reality they will pass very quickly, especially as the time will be spread over several months.

Your coursework will allow you to demonstrate your skills in textiles, so you need to select your project carefully in order to gain the most marks.

Your coursework is comprised of two parts.

The design folder

Designing skills account for 40 per cent of the coursework marks. Your design folder will tell the story of how you have progressed from your design brief to your final product. It carries all the evidence of the work you have done. It also shows how well you can communicate your ideas through a variety of different media such as drawing, narrative, spreadsheets and photographs. The design folder needs to be set out in a logical order, clearly following the design process. You could also use a GANTT chart to show your planning.

Remember, marks for the quality of written evidence are included in this section so you are advised to check your work carefully for spelling, punctuation and grammar, as well as the correct use of technical terms.

The practical outcome

Making skills account for 60 per cent of your coursework marks. The practical outcome demonstrates your ability to produce a well-finished, marketable product. It also shows the range of skills that you have mastered.

Making includes all the preparatory work, such as testing fabrics for suitability, trying out different seams, and checking the fit of the final piece of work. It also includes the actual making up of the final item and the designing of patterns, motifs and colourways on the computer. In order to achieve well in this section, you must demonstrate a range of different skills (you will not be penalised, however, if you do not use a computer in your making).

Remember, the finish of all work should be to the highest quality possible. You need to aim for a good range of skills that you can complete well rather than a very wide range that you cannot achieve well.

What's in this section?

* ★ **8.1** The design process
* ★ **8.2** Choosing a project outline and planning your time
* ★ **8.3** Task analysis and research
* ★ **8.4** Design specification and design ideas
* ★ **8.5** Developing a solution and planning the making
* ★ **8.6** The manufacturing specification
* ★ **8.7** Evaluating your product

In this chapter you will:

★   learn about the design process

★   understand how to lay out your design folder clearly.

The design process

The design process follows the development of the product from the design brief through to the final product. It should clearly show the constraints of the design brief and how they have been met, as well as all the stages of development through the testing of ideas and techniques to the final product.

For example, it is important that the fastenings for a child's garment have been tested with a child of the appropriate age so that if the fastenings were found to be too small and fiddly, the feedback would indicate a different, larger, solution. This type of feedback shows your understanding of what you have learned and your knowledge of how to correct it.

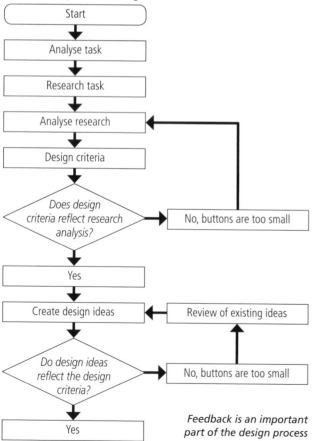

Feedback is an important part of the design process

Each aspect of the design process needs to be checked against your own knowledge and the results of your investigations. You also need to keep checking the criteria for each grade as given by the examination board.

Layout

Your design folder should be laid out in a logical way so that the reader can easily follow the steps that you have taken. If it is not clear, you may lose marks. Remember to give the reasons why you have made your decision, such as which fabric or which seam was chosen. Other hints on laying out your design folder include:

*   be precise and concise – only include relevant information, such as the results of the research that have helped you make your decisions
*   tell the story so that others can see how your project has developed
*   keep your work neat, but remember there are no marks given for decorating pages
*   plan your pages carefully and do not waste space
*   refer back to your design brief and design criteria to ensure that you keep focused on the task – if you need to make a change, then justify it
*   remember there are marks for the Quality of Written Communication. Spell check your work and try to use the correct terminology at all times
*   check that you are using a good variety of appropriate skills in the practical work
*   make sure that you understand what you need to include to reach each grade. The clearer and better organized your work is, the higher your grade is likely to be.

Summary

★   The design process tracks the development of the product from the design brief to the final product.

★   The design folder should be laid out in a logical and accessible way.

★   All aspects of the design process should be checked against existing knowledge, feedback and the examination criteria.

8.2 Choosing a project outline and planning your time

In this chapter you will:
★ learn how to choose a project outline and to plan your time effectively.

Project outline

Choosing the right project is essential to your success. AQA offer a list of suggestions in the subject specification. Your teacher may decide which of these to offer as the best suited to you, or you may be offered a free choice. In some cases, your teacher may write a design brief with you to suit your individual needs.

Before starting work on any project, it is a good idea to do an ideas map of what is required for the project. This will help to clarify your thoughts and may even lead to a change of mind – better now than when you have done a lot of work. An ideas map is a useful tool to help you at many different stages in your work and will help you plan your research. This is explained in the next chapter.

Your teacher will be able to advise you about the facilities available in school. It would be unwise to plan to include elaborate machine embroidery, for example, if you do not have a machine capable of doing it.

Remember that whichever design brief you choose you will be working on it for some time, so you need to be really interested in it! You also need to remember that this is the showcase for your skills, so you need to demonstrate your expertise and not necessarily go for the simplest and easiest option.

Planning your time

As you will be working within a tight time frame, it is a good idea to plan your time by using a GANTT chart to plot your activities (see page 126 for an example or a GANTT chart). You can use this type of chart to sequence all the tasks you must carry out during the design process. By writing the activities in the vertical column and showing the 40 hours broken down into chunks along the horizontal, you can see how long each activity will take.

You can also use this type of chart to plan the production of your final product.

Summary

★ It is very important to choose the right project for your coursework, bearing in mind your own capabilities and the facilities available to you.

★ Drawing an ideas map is a very useful tool in clarifying your thoughts and ideas before you start work on the project.

★ Careful planning of your time with the aid of a GANTT chart will ensure that you cover all the tasks in the design process within the allotted time.

Doing your coursework project

Task analysis and research

In this part of your coursework you must:

A GRADE Analyse the task and the research material logically, thoroughly and effectively.

C GRADE Analyse the task and the research material.

E GRADE Make a superficial analysis of the task and most of the research material.

Task analysis

Once you have chosen the brief that interests you most, you will need to look carefully at exactly what you are being asked to do. An ideas map or spider diagram is a very good way to do this. Begin by identifying the key words in the design brief. Look at this example: 'Design and make a garment for a toddler using denim.'

The key terms here are 'toddler' and 'denim'. These two words tell you the age group and the fabric for the product, and will help you to develop some ideas for products. In turn, this will help identify what kind of research you need to do before developing your design brief.

The task analysis should consider all aspects of the task and so it should include:

- the design of the garment
- the making of the garment
- time management
- where and how to gather more information
- methods of making
- marketing.

You will need to think about:

- *who* the product is for
- *what* it is for
- *when* it will be used
- *how* it will be used
- *where* it will be sold
- *why* it is needed.

The answers to these questions form the task analysis.

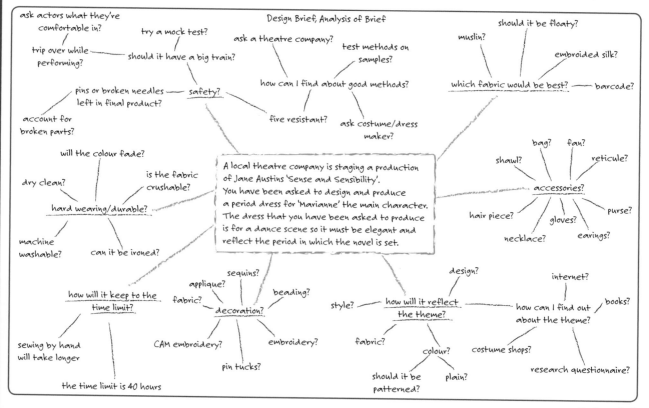

Task analysis

Research and analysis

In this part of your coursework you must:

A GRADE Use a wide variety of appropriate sources to gather relevant research information.

C GRADE Use a variety of appropriate sources to gather and order relevant research information.

E GRADE Use a limited number of sources to gather research information

See also the grades box on page 138.

Your research should help you to find out information that will make it easier to design textiles products required by your design brief.

Research

Your research must be relevant to the task. For example, if you already know that the fabric is denim and the target group is toddlers, there is no point in researching alternative fabrics and garments for other age groups. List what you know and then list what you need to find out. Think about your customers. Who wears the clothes and who pays for them? You may find that the purchasers and the wearers are different people and have different requirements. How would you find this out? Refer back to your design brief and task analysis. It is important to keep reminding yourself exactly what it is that you are trying to achieve.

Some examples of useful forms of research include:

- consumer surveys: you should not include the questionnaire itself in the project, just the findings presented in chart form together with a summary of the findings
- Internet and CD-ROMs: show how you have used the information and not just include printouts
- product analysis: looking at an existing product to see how well it is suited for the intended client
- mood board: this must be relevant, usually A4 or A3 sized and must contain the reasons for including it. It may be better used to help you with your design ideas, but it can be a source of research

Mood boards can help with both design ideas and research

- fabric samples: showing the type of fabrics that may be suitable for your product
- samples of techniques: this type of research may be included later in the development of your product.

Analysing your research

You should analyse the information you find during your research, saying how it has helped you, what conclusions you can draw from it and how you will use it to write your design specification and produce your design ideas. You do not need to include all your research in your project folder. Instead you should just record the results and analysis of it. Merely printing out information from the Internet or including photocopies will not be awarded any marks.

Presentation of research

This section of your folder gives many opportunities to display your ICT skills in the way you present your findings; marks are awarded for this. Questionnaire results can be presented in graph form using Excel and chart wizard, even if they are small. Attribute profiles can be reproduced at a small size. You could also show how you have used information from the Internet or CD-ROMs and not just include printouts.

Make sure that your research is precise and concise. Your research should only take up two to three pages of your project folder. Remember that you may add to your research later in your project where relevant.

Summary

★ In order to understand the design brief you must analyse it carefully.

★ You need to keep the research relevant to your design brief.

★ Remember to present only the results of your research.

Analysing fabric samples

Design specification and design ideas

In this part of your coursework you must:

A GRADE Produce a detailed specification that focuses closely on the design brief and analysis of research.

C GRADE Produce a specification that reflects the design brief and analysis of research.

E GRADE Produce a specification that reflects the most obvious features of the analysis.

Design specification

The design criteria specification is a list of features (design criteria) that your product will have. Your design specification must reflect the analysis of your research otherwise you have nothing on which to base your ideas. It is helpful if your criteria are clearly laid out, using subheadings and bullet points. Your specification should show the essential characteristics of your design as well as the desirable ones.

For example:
- the target market: who the product is aimed at
- the timescale for making it

Design Specification

Here is the design specification for evening wear to present to the company 'Out of the East'.

Function: -
- It must come in a variety of sizes if it was mass produced
- It must be comfortable and durable
- It must be easily washable and ironed easily
- The colour of the material must not fade or transfer onto other material
- It must not crease easily

Appearance: -
- The colour range must tie in with the oriental theme
- The decoration must reflect the oriental theme
- The garment must look good for formal occasions
- The design or decoration, if any, must be reasonably small and should be interesting
- The garment must fit nicely to the correct size

Part of a design specification

- the type of production: one-off, batch or mass production
- the quality of the product: whether it should be washable
- the size of the product
- the finish of the product: does it need decoration and, if so, what type?
- the type or types of fabric to be used
- whether the design has a one-way pattern to it, such as flowers growing
- the cost of the materials and components.

Design ideas

In this part of your coursework you must:

A GRADE Produce a wide range of distinct proposals which satisfy the specification.

C GRADE Produce a range of proposals which satisfy the specification.

E GRADE Produce some proposals which satisfy most of the specification.

Your design specification should enable you to create a range of design ideas for a product to meet the needs of the design brief. For example, you could design a range of cushions using different fabrics and design techniques in order to demonstrate your designing and making skills.

In order to gain the higher grades for this section, you must fully annotate all your designs, including as much detail as possible about fabrics and techniques and justifying how each idea fits the design criteria in your specification. You then need to evaluate your design ideas. You could use a table to check each design against the design criteria, using either ticks or a mark out of five, or a combination of both (see opposite).

You should refer to the ways in which your product contributes to environmental issues. Green issues are becoming more and more important and you may consider using fibres from vegetable or renewable sources and avoiding those made from animal or chemical sources. Is it possible to recycle your product and, if so, in which ways? You may also include the effects of some fabrics on the working environment. Fur fabric can be very difficult to work with as it creates a lot of dust, which could affect asthmatics.

Doing your coursework project

Design criteria	Design 1	Design 2	Design 3	Design 4	Design 5	Design 6	Design 7
1 Washable fabric (mark out of 5 for how easily the fabric washes)	5	3	4	0	5	4	2
2 Decorative finish	✓	✓	✓	✓	✓	✓	✓
3 Number of different fabrics used	2	5	3	6	2	3	3
4 Removable cover	✓	✓	✓	✓	✓	✓	✓
5 Non-directional design (the pattern or design does not have to be seen from one direction)	✓	✓	✓	✓	✓	✓	✓

Evaluating design ideas using a table

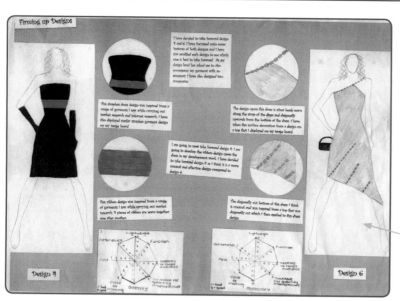

A range of design ideas

If at any stage of your work you change or modify it, then you must record the information. This will provide the record to show how you arrived at your final solution.

Computer aided design (CAD)

In this part of your coursework you must:

A GRADE Select and skillfully use a wide range of communication, graphical and ICT skills to convey ideas effectively and precisely.

C GRADE Use a range of communication, graphical and ICT skills to convey ideas effectively.

E GRADE Use some appropriate communication, graphical and ICT skills to convey ideas.

You can use a computer to help generate design through:

- ClipArt – adapting or changing the ClipArt to fit your design ideas
- drawing programmes
- printing onto transfer paper (the design can be transferred onto the fabric by ironing)
- specialist software that will allow you to design clothes, patterns and colourways
- software to demonstrate the best pattern layouts.

It is a good idea to indicate how these techniques could be used to help produce your designs. Where possible, you should include your own examples, but if you do not have the facilities available, explain how they could be used. Later in your work you will need to show how they could be used to help in the mass production of your product.

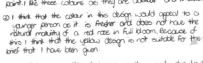

This piece shows good use of CAD to aid the colour selection and it is well annotated.

This piece shows good use of CAD but would have benefited from more annotation. The machine embroidery is an example of CAM but does not fit the theme very well.

CAD can be a useful tool for developing your design ideas

Summary

★ Your design specification should include both essential and desirable criteria.

★ Remember to check your design ideas against your design sepcification.

★ Try to include the use of CAD in your design ideas.

8.5 Developing a solution and planning the making

In this part of your coursework you must:

A GRADE Use one or more of your proposals and relevant knowledge of techniques, manufacturing and working characteristics to develop a detailed and coherent design solution.

C GRADE Use your proposals and relevant knowledge to develop a detailed design solution which satisfies the specification.

E GRADE Use your own proposals and relevant knowledge to produce a solution which satisfies most of the specification.

Included in your making marks are activities such as planning your time, testing fabrics for suitability for the task, and techniques to find the most appropriate for the task.

Developing a solution

When you have evaluated your design ideas against the design specification, you need to select the one that best fits the design specification. You need to show clearly how you have arrived at your final choices. Remember that you are 'telling the story' of how you arrived at your final solution to someone who has not seen the work in progress.

Throughout your work you will need to find the best way of completing each process in the making. This will prove that you have understood the requirements of the specification and have made the best choices for your product. You will need to think about each step that you take, from the choice of the fabric to the type of seam to be used or the type of fastening that is most suitable.

For example:
- is your fabric suitable
- are your seams suitable
- is your decoration appropriate for the fabric/garment
- what type of decoration is required
- how are you shaping the garment
- does it need interfacing, lining, support for embroidery
- does it need fastenings
- what kind of hem is best?

Modifications

In this part of your coursework you must:

A GRADE Record and justify the need for any changes or adaptations.

C GRADE Recognize the need for and justify any changes or adaptations.

E GRADE Correct working errors where necessary.

During the designing and planning stages, you should have recorded and justified any modifications you made to your design or pattern. You will either need to buy or make a pattern. If you have bought a commercial pattern, you need to check that it fits properly, perhaps by making a toile.

Changes to the pattern count as modifications, so you need to make detailed notes on what you have done and most importantly why you have done it. This will show your knowledge and understanding of your project. If you do not do this, you will limit the marks that you receive for this section of your work. If you want to achieve a high grade, then you must explain the modifications that you make. This is made very clear in the marking criteria, grade C requires modifications to be recorded and justified.

Planning for manufacture

In this part of your coursework you must:

A GRADE Produce a correct sequence of activities that show where, why and how practical production decisions were made.

C GRADE Plan a largely correct, and workable, sequence of main making activities.

E GRADE Demonstrate some forward planning.

When you have selected your most suitable design idea, you need to plan the tasks involved in its production. Do this in note form to begin with.

When making a plan for production, it is helpful to draw a flow diagram of the processes involved in making your product, using the notes that you have been keeping to help you. Think about the quality controls that you will need to include; for example, checking the width of seams to see that they are within the tolerances; if not, the product will not be the right size. This is a **critical control** and ensures that the product is workable. You need to show these controls in your flow diagram. Remember that this must include the steps carried out, decisions made and feedback to the system.

Summary

★ To gain a high grade you must show how you have modified your product.

★ You must record all your modifications.

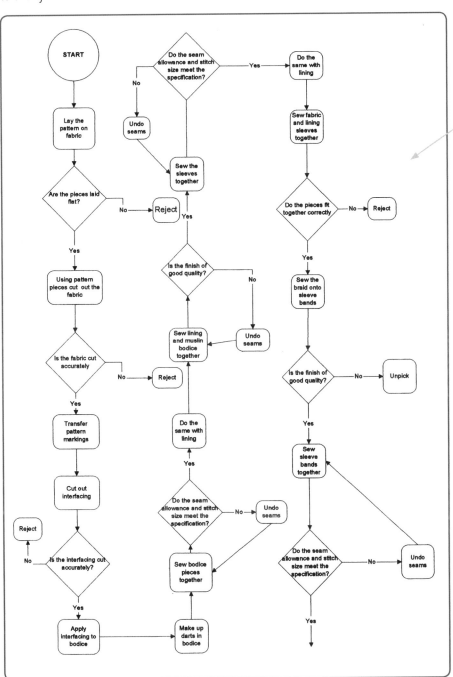

This is a good flowchart with detailed step-by-step instructions, quality controls and feedback

A plan for production in the form of a flow chart

Doing your coursework project

The manufacturing specification

In this part of your coursework you must:

A GRADE Be logical and clear, and include detailed feedback, and details of quality control and quality assurance.

C GRADE Be logical and include details of quality control and quality assurance.

E GRADE Make a simple attempt at a manufacturing specification.

A manufacturing specification tells a manufacturer exactly how to produce the product. It is a very detailed document, which should include:

- the total time for the project, the GANTT chart. This needs to be realistic. Remember that you only have 40 hours for the full course and 20 for the short course
- a materials and components list
- a production plan including details of:
  - the tools to be used
  - quality assurance
  - quality control
- the fabric to be used: fibre, weave, width, quality, cost, colour, handle, washability, aftercare (samples of the fabric to be used would be included)
- the pattern to be used
- tolerances
- pattern layout and means of cutting
- processes to be used appropriate for the type of production: one-off, batch production or mass production
- details of where CAM can be used in production
- the time taken for each process to be completed
- health and safety measures, such as accounting for all broken needles to ensure they are not left in a product
- a production system, including all controls and feedback into the system
- details of any packaging, as appropriate, such as for mail order product
- key issues you faced during designing or making
- where computers could be used to aid mass production; examples could include computerized weaving or knitting of fabric, printing patterns
- spreadsheets showing the scaling-up of costing and quantity.

Part of a manufacturing specification for a dress

Evaluating your product

> In this part of your coursework you must:
> **A GRADE** Test, objectively evaluate and effectively modify your work throughout the process as appropriate.
> **C GRADE** Test, evaluate and modify your work throughout the process as appropriate.
> **E GRADE** Test and evaluate some aspects of your work.

When you have completed your coursework and produced a final product, you must do one more thing: write a final evaluation. This is a summative evaluation; it rounds off your coursework and 'finishes the story'. It explains how successful your final product is – if it matches the specifications.

You need to remember that this means referring back to your design brief and to your specification in order to see how well your product matches them. This is not a diary of what you did and whether you are pleased with the end product. You should have tested your product to ensure that it matches the criteria given. For example, if your specification states that your product must have a machine-embroidered pocket, state whether it has and, if not, say why not. Is the size correct? Does it meet the tolerances given? Is the fabric suitable? Have you kept within the costing? What do other people think of your product, particularly potential users? If you had to make the product again, what modifications would you make?

Finally, look back. Have you told the story of your product from your design brief through to your final product, showing how you arrived there and giving the reasons for your decisions? If you have, well done; you should do well.

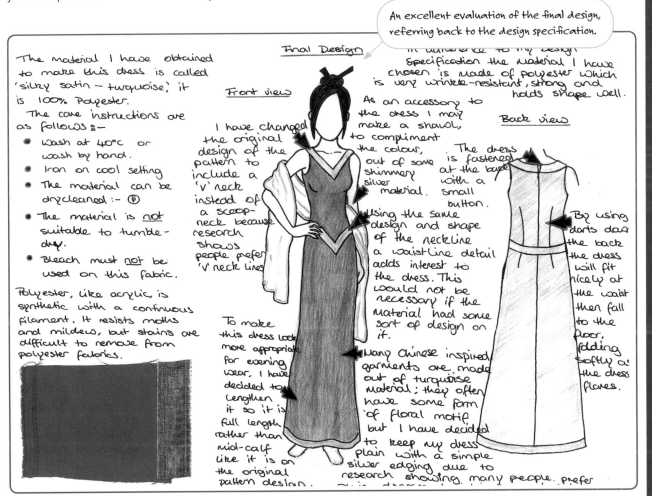

> An excellent evaluation of the final design, referring back to the design specification.

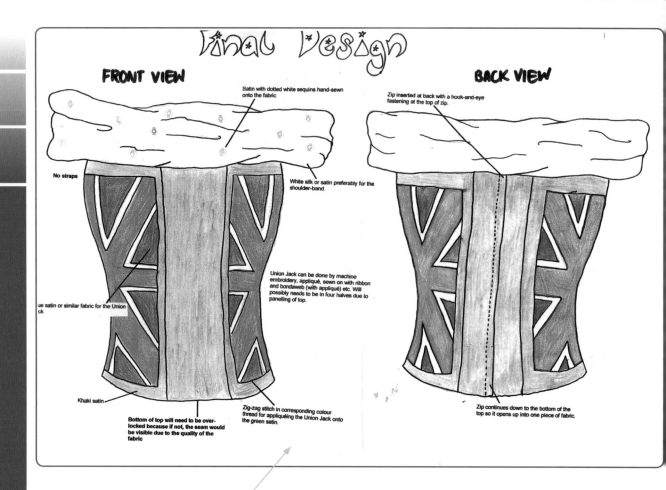

Final Design

FRONT VIEW

No straps

Satin with dotted white sequins hand-sewn onto the fabric

White silk or satin preferably for the shoulder-band.

ue satin or similar fabric for the Union ck

Union Jack can be done by machine embroidery, appliqué, sewn on with ribbon and bondaweb (with appliqué) etc. Will possibly needs to be in four halves due to panelling of top.

Khaki satin

Bottom of top will need to be over-locked because if not, the seam would be visible due to the quality of the fabric

Zig-zag stitch in corresponding colour thread for appliquéing the Union Jack onto the green satin.

BACK VIEW

Zip inserted at back with a hook-and-eye fastening at the top of zip.

Zip continues down to the bottom of the top so it opens up into one piece of fabric.

This is more of a description of the product and it does not refer back to the design specification. More marks would be gained by referring closely to the specification.

Summary

★ The manufacturing specification must:
  - be logical
  - be clear
  - include feedback
  - include quality assurance and quality control measures.

9 Preparing for the exam

The examination carries 40 per cent of your total marks and is split into foundation and higher tiers. This means that you cannot achieve lower than a grade D on the higher tier paper. If you receive fewer marks than that – other than a very few marks at the very top of the E band – you will automatically receive a U grade. The highest grade possible on the foundation paper is a grade C. It is important that you discuss the entry level with your teacher so that you understand which tier you have been entered for and why. There are many similarities between the two papers, but the higher tier offers more opportunities for the expansion of responses.

Before going into more detail about the examination, here are some useful tips.

★ Generally, students achieve better results in their coursework than in their exam, often 1 to 2 grades higher.

★ Marks are frequently lost in the exam through not answering the question that has been asked.

★ The exam tests very similar skills and topics to the coursework, but students often do not make the connections.

★ Using the correct terminology for tools, fabrics, fibres and processes in your answers will gain marks.

★ Answers need to be precise and concise; you can lose the thread of what you are trying to say if you waffle.

★ Practise answering past exam questions; this will help you interpret the questions on your paper and also give you confidence.

★ Planning what you want to include in your answer will help you focus; you could use the left-hand margin for this. Also, if you have a plan and do not have time to complete your answer, you may at least get some marks for the plan.

What's in this section?

★ **9.1** The preparation sheet

★ **9.2** Preparation for the exam

★ **9.3** Examination technique

The preparation sheet

In this chapter you will:

★ learn how to use the preparation sheet to guide you in your revision.

Prior to the examination, usually at the beginning of March, you will be given the exam preparation sheet. This gives you the *focus* for your revision but does *not* mean that other areas covered by the specification will not come up in the exam.

The inspirational theme

The preparation sheet gives you the inspirational theme, in the case of the 2003 exam, the theme was 'insects'.

The research context

You are also given the research context, in this case FASHIONABLE CLOTHING or DECORATIVE INTERIOR PRODUCTS. The research context advises you of the type of products that you will be questioned about designing and making.

You are always given a choice of products; of these you choose one to research. This is followed by about six bullet points for you to consider and there is also an extension activity for those students taking the higher tier paper. The extension activity allows higher tier candidates to develop their theme and to demonstrate their understanding of the function of materials.

Getting started

You may find it helpful to make a mood board to help you focus your thoughts on the inspirational theme and the research context. For this you could collect pictures and drawings of insects and look at how they could influence the shape or decoration of fashionable clothing or a decorative interior product.

In the exam, you will need to be able to produce two designs that meet the design criteria given. It is a good idea to think of some designs and practise them so that you are fully familiar with them. Having coloured pens or pencils in the exam can help in laying out your ideas.

Analysing the preparation sheet

When you receive your preparation sheet, you should analyse it carefully to help you prepare for the exam. It is a good idea to look at a previous year's preparation sheets and the exam papers. This will help you see how the preparation sheet feeds into the exam paper. It will also show just how important it is to fully prepare yourself. Opposite you will see the preparation sheet from the 2003 exam, along with examples of how this could have been analysed.

Other elements on the preparation sheet

There is usually some extra information for students taking the higher-mark paper or for those taking the full course rather than the short course. Make sure you identify this part of the sheet and check with your teacher whether you need to revise this.

On the 2003 preparation sheet, students are asked to investigate manipulating fabrics into 3D effects. You might think about using quilting for bodies or wiring to make freestanding wings. You need to show that you understand the meaning of 3D as well as showing your understanding of how different types and weights of fabric may be manipulated.

You cannot take any of this research or preparation work into the exam. However, the work that you do will still be very important to you in the exam. If you are well prepared and have followed the instructions of the preparation sheet, you will be able to answer questions and apply your knowledge easily.

Summary

★ The exam preparation sheet gives you a focus for your revision, but does not include everything you need to revise.

★ The exam preparation sheet gives you the inspirational theme and the research context for the exam.

★ Analysing the exam preparation sheet is an important starting point in your revision process.

The 2003 preparation sheet included visual images of insects. This indicated that these would form the basis for any designs produced, to be used in either clothing or decorative interior products. The sheet also states that a designer would produce a mood board, so it would be wise to prepare for the exam by making a mood board to help you think of some design ideas.

The next point was to investigate product design and manufacture for either fashionable tops OR decorative interior products for use on chairs. This would indicate chair covers or cushions as the most likely option for interior products. There is also no need to consider trousers or skirts as only tops have been specified.

You are asked to produce some initial designs which could be developed in the examination. It is a good idea to do this preliminary work so that you have the designs already worked out and you are familiar with them. This will save you time in the exam and will also allow you to take advice from your teacher about your designs that will not be available to you during the exam.

General Certificate of Secondary Education
Summer 2003
Foundation and Higher Examination

PREPARATION SHEET FOR THE 2003 EXAMINATION 3547/57PM

Design and Technology: Textiles Technology
*(For the Foundation and Higher Tiers of the
Short and Full Courses)*

Instructions
- This Preparation Sheet will be given to you on or after 1 March 2003. The context for some of the examination questions is given below.
- Between 1 March and the examination date you will have the opportunity to research the context with the guidance of your teacher.
- **No Preparation Sheets or any associated material may be taken into the examination room.**

INSPIRATIONAL THEME:	INSECTS
RESEARCH CONTEXT:	FASHIONABLE CLOTHING *OR* DECORATIVE INTERIOR PRODUCTS

Study the points below.

A designer would put together a mood board as a source of inspiration.

- Research visual images associated with insects.
- Investigate product design and manufacture in one of the following areas:

    (i) fashionable tops **or**

    (ii) decorative interior products for use on chairs.

- Produce some initial designs which you can develop into final products in the examination.
- Investigate the types of fibres, fabrics and components appropriate to the research context.
- Investigate the ways in which these textile products can be manufactured.
- Investigate ways in which ICT might be used in the design and manufacture of these products.

    For the Higher Tier papers you should also investigate ways of manipulating fabrics in order to give 3-dimensional effects.

TT/0203/3547/57PM   6/6   **Turn over ▶**

The preparation sheet for the 2003 exam

The final point that applies to both tiers tells the student to investigate the ways in which ICT could be used in the design and manufacture of their products. This includes all forms of ICT, from presenting and storing data gathered, to manufacturing using CAD and CAM. However, it must be related to the products.

When doing your research, you should also think about how to manufacture your chosen product, including all the controls and safety factors.

Here you are told to investigate the types of fibres, fabrics and components appropriate for the research context. You will be asked about these, possibly relating to your design, but not necessarily so. For this inspirational theme and research context, it would be sensible to look at, for example, gauzy fabrics that could represent wings, or plastic or leather type fabrics which could represent the scaly body of an insect. You might also think about the items suitable for manufacturing tops or decorative interior products.

Preparation for the exam

In this chapter you will:

★ learn how to produce a revision plan and revise successfully.

When you start your preparation for the exam, the first point you need to remember is that this is not your only exam, so you need to share time equally between all of your subjects. Also bear in mind that you should:

- start preparing early
- produce a revision plan and stick to it
- revise thoroughly and frequently: little and often is a good rule – 15 minutes at a time is about right. Have a short break after 15 minutes and then come back to it
- go over each topic several times
- practise the designs that you have produced from the preparation sheet so that you can replicate them easily
- drink plenty of water to oxygenate your brain; this will help you to remember things more easily
- remember that the exam will test the same sorts of topics as your coursework so you already have a lot of knowledge.

Prepare a revision plan

Write your plan out on paper. The plan should include:
- all your examination dates
- any remaining coursework deadlines
- study leave
- extra lessons in school
- personal or family occasions, such as birthdays
- some time for relaxation and exercise – you will learn and remember more if you do this.

Once you have added all these things to your plan, you need to divide the remaining time up between the subjects that you are taking. When allocating time to each subject, it is a good idea to take into account the following:
- your mock examination results. If you did not do as well as you expected in your mock, do you need to spend extra time revising for this subject?
- how important is the subject to you and your future plans?
- how easy do you find the subject?
- the date of the examination.

Try to stick closely to your plan but remember that you can change it.

Revision methods

We all have different methods of revision and you will need to find the best one for you. Think about how you learn. Do you learn best though reading, listening, seeing or doing? You should give this some thought and then use the information. For example, if you learn by listening, get someone to help by reading to you. If you learn by doing, try making a mock-up of your design ideas.

When revising, you need to be comfortable but focused. It is a good idea to let your family and friends know when you are working so that you are not disturbed.

Try using several different methods of revision:
- reading: silently or aloud
- listening: get someone to read to you or try associating background music with different topics; remember the music and you will remember the topic
- making notes from textbooks or from your own notes: read them and then try to reproduce them without looking at the originals
- spider diagrams or mind-mapping: a good technique for learning the key words connected to a topic
- drawing, sketching: you need to be able to reproduce the designs you have created
- trying out some of the textile techniques you have included in your designs: make a mock-up or toile
- use past papers to time yourself on different questions: the design question usually carries about a third of the marks and so should take about a third of the time
- use a friend or relative to test you on different topics.

Summary

★ Make a revision plan and stick to it!

★ Do not rely on just learning facts – this is not enough for success in textiles.

9.3 Examination technique

> **In this chapter you will:**
> ★ learn how to answer the exam questions.

The table below shows the time allotted to the full and short course exam papers, higher and foundation tiers.

Course	Examination paper	Time
Full course	Higher tier	2 hours
	Foundation tier	$1\frac{1}{2}$ hours
Short course	Higher tier	$1\frac{1}{2}$
	Foundation tier	$1\frac{1}{2}$

Before you start the examination, you need to read the front of the exam paper. Check the following.
- Are you in the correct tier of entry?
- Do you have the correct equipment?
- Make sure that you understand all the instructions.
- Read the information given and make sure that you understand it.
- Check that you have any figure drawing outlines provided with the exam paper.

Next, read the paper through carefully, taking particular note of the design brief given at the start of the paper. This will be closely related to the inspirational theme and the research context from the preparation sheet.

It is a good idea to answer questions in the order that they appear on the paper. This is because you have a focus for the paper and it will follow the same order as the design process in your folder.

At the beginning of each question you will be given the focus for the question, and you should read this carefully. Next, read the question carefully and work out what each question is asking you, for example:
- *describe* means talk about; *describe* a technique means say how and why it is carried out. This can include sketches or diagrams.
- *give a suggestion for the type of fabric* means name the type of fabric and say what it is like, and you may want to highlight specific properties
- *explain* means that you need to expand your answer with reasons. You may also be asked for more than one

reason. If you only give one, you have halved your marks!
- *develop* means that you need to thoroughly explain and expand – usually on a preliminary idea
- *evaluate* means look at it critically; what are the strengths and weaknesses; compare with the design criteria
- do *not* give one word answers unless you are only asked to name something. You should apply your knowledge. For example, polar fleece would be a suitable fabric for a baby blanket *because* it is soft and easily washed
- make sure that you annotate all designs that you create
- be concise and do not waffle.

Underline the key words in the question to make sure that you focus on the right points in your answer and keep referring to the design brief as most of the paper relates to this. You should also note the amount of space and the number of marks given for each part of the question. These give an indication of how much information is required.

The design question

This question carries approximately one third of the total marks for the exam. To begin with, you need to refer back to the design brief given at the start of the paper. Look at the example below.

> **Design brief**
> You are the designer for a manufacturing company. A client has asked you to use inspiration from the shape, pattern, colours and texture of insects to design and make an original and exciting product that will sell well.
>
> Choose **one** of the following:
> **Either** (a) a fashion top **or** (b) a product for use on a chair in a living room.
>
> - The product will be batch produced.
> - The product must be based on the shapes, patterns, colours and textures linked with insects.
> - The product must have an interesting feature made from fabric you have manipulated.
>
> (AQA 2003, Higher Paper)

Preparing for the exam

You will probably be asked to produce **two** design ideas to meet this brief and then to choose one of them. To gain full marks, they must be significantly different and well annotated. The rest of this question will relate to the idea that you choose, so be sure that you have not drawn something that you are not familiar with. If you have produced design ideas from the preparation sheet, use them here.

Throughout this question the marks are clearly indicated. Remember, marks are only awarded once for each point made. You must ensure that you make lots of *different* points and not just repeat the same one.

d Use sketches, labelling and notes to present a final design for your product.
You have this page and the next to present your design.
If you have chosen the fashion top, you may use the body shapes as a guide.
Marks will be awarded for:
- choice of suitable fabrics/components
  (4 marks)
- manipulation of fabric *(3 marks)*
- use of colour in the product *(4 marks)*
- quality of the design and use of shapes, patterns and textures linked with insects
  (8 marks)
- presentation of the final idea. *(3 marks)*
(AQA 2003, Higher Paper)

In order to achieve maximum marks, you must be clear and precise.

Marks will be awarded for:
- choice of suitable fabrics/components *(4 marks)*

Exam Hint
Make a good choice of fabric: perhaps cotton voile for the wings because it is very light and fine; shiny PVC for the body because it is leathery in appearance. Components used might be small round beads mounted on fine wire for the antennae and to edge the wings because they will tremble and appear life-like; a nylon zipper to close the back of the cushion. NB this would not be suitable for a small child.

Marks will be awarded for:
- manipulation of fabric *(3 marks)*

Exam Hint
The voile for the wings could be tie dyed and then pleated where they join the body. The PVC for the body might be quilted into scales and then have extra padding underneath to raise it before being appliquéd to the cushion.

Marks will be awarded for:
- use of colour in the product *(4 marks)*

Exam Hint
Here, your sketch would have to show all the colours used. You may also add the reasons for the colours such as 'the PVC will be black with red circles appliquéd onto it to represent the colours of the ladybird'.

Marks will be awarded for:
- quality of the design and use of shapes, patterns and textures linked with insects
  (4 marks)
- presentation of the final idea. *(3 marks)*

Exam Hint
To gain full marks here you must:
- show clear detail related to the specification
- produce a quality drawing
- be imaginative
- show how your design is suitable for the purpose
- show the use of shape, pattern and texture and relate them to the focus
- use the space on the product to advantage; a well-placed and sized design
- show how the product could be made in quantity. How could you manage the extra padding easily for batch production?
- present your ideas clearly with care; include front and back views as well as, perhaps, an exploded view or extra sketches of the detail.

Glossary

abrasion the wearing away of a textile by friction as you could find on the elbows and knees of garments

achromatic black, grey or white

advertising any form of media which informs and influences existing or new customers

aesthetics how a fabric looks

annotation adding notes to diagrams and drawings to explain and develop the ideas further

appliqué a technique of decorating fabric by combining textiles in an interesting pattern and applying them to a background

basic block a two-dimensional shape, formed from a detailed set of measurements, which are produced for each section of a garment; the starting point for producing a pattern for clothing

batch dyeing a method of dyeing fabric in which a batch of fabric is held in a dyeing machine with the dye; it may be fixed in the same machine

batik a method of dyeing fabric using a resist to stop the dye being absorbed on certain areas of the fabric and so creating a pattern

BEAB British Electrotechnical Approvals Board

bespoke a single product which is specially made or made to order

bias the diagonal of the woven fabric

biopolishing a process of fabric finishing, which takes place before the fabric is dyed, in which the fabric is treated quickly with enzymes when wet to help remove short fibre ends and make the fabric smoother and less likely to pill

biostoning a process of fabric finishing, which takes place after dyeing, to give a faded look to denim products

bonded a non-woven fabric in which layers of fibres are laid down in a web and strengthened by bonding

CAD computer aided design

CAM computer aided manufacture

card reader a small card that can be inserted into a computer for transferring designs to a sewing machine

cellulose the material that all plants are made of

CE mark a sign that shows that the product meets the relevant EU (European Union) Directive for safety

chromatic textiles textiles that change colour according to the environment and the wearer

closed questions questions included in a questionnaire which ask people to select an answer from a range of given answers

components items that are used in the construction of the finished textile product, such as zips, buttons, Velcro and braid

conformance the costs of producing high quality goods with very few faults

consumption the process in which items are used up

cording the process of trapping a cord between two layers of fabric then securing it using stitching

critical control the quality controls required in production to ensure that the product is workable

darts method of making a garment fit closely by folding the fabric and then sewing it in place

database a record or list contain information of a certain type

design brief a key document that is drawn up by the client to guide the designer in the design process

design inspiration

design specification a series of requirements that set the restrictions within which designers work

desirable criteria elements that a designer would like the design specification to have

devoré a technique that involves printing a mixed fabric, such as viscose and silk, with a chemical that takes away the silk or the viscose in that section leaving a design in relief and a fine gauze in between

direct the costs of materials, components and labour involved in making a product

durability toughness, resilience, strength, hard wearing properties of a fabric

efficiency a means of using resources in the manufacturing process to minimize costs and to reduce wastage

effluent waste dye and water from the manufacturing process

essential criteria elements that the design specification must have

evaluation assessing whether each step of the production process works well and efficiently without introducing any faults or errors

exclusive designs only suitable for certain groups or ages

felted a non-woven fabric in which layers of fibres are laid down in a web and strengthened by felting

fibre blend a fibre made by mixing two or more fibres together before the fibre is spun into a yarn

fibre mixture (union) a fabric made by mixing two or more different yarns

filament long textile fibres; fabrics such as linen and silk are made up of these

finish a thickening agent to make the fabric stiffer while printing

flammability the propensity of a material to catch fire

flow chart (system diagram) a diagram of a production process showing where decisions are made, quality control checks are carried out and how the feedback re-informs the system

form shape, appearance, structure of a product

formative evaluation evaluation of a design that takes place at each stage of the designer's work

free form embroidery a type of machine embroidery, using satin stitch or straight stitch, which allows the operator to decide in which direction the stitching will go and how it will look

GANTT chart a table listing all the processes involved in producing a product and the time allocated to each process, showing whether any processes will overlap and whether your production process will fit in the time allowed

gathers a means by which the fullness of a fabric can be reduced using small stitches that can be pulled up to reduce the length of the fabric

generic general, broad, common

grain the warp yarns that run the length of the fabric

grey goods fabrics before they are finished and made up into textiles products

handle how a fabric feels

hazards a step or process that could cause harm at work

ICT information and communication technology

inclusive designs that can be used by all people

indirect costs the hidden costs involved in making a product such as research and development, advertising and transport

Ingeo a substance made from plant starches, which fully biodegrades into natural ingredients that add nutrition to the soil

inorganic derived from non-living things

ISO 9000 a quality assurance mark

Jacquard loom a type of loom used to create complex weaves

lay plan (cutting layout) an arrangement of the pattern pieces on the fabric to ensure the best use of the material

legislation making laws to protect the safety and the interests of the consumer

line one of the key principles of design. Line may refer to the fabric design or the shape of a garment

machine embroidery thread a very fine thread with a high sheen, usually silk, viscose, rayon, or low twist polyester, used for machine embroidery

manipulate a way of handling a flat fabric in order to change it into a shaped product

manufacturing specification a detailed specification written once the final product has been developed, which explains exactly what the product is and how it will be made

marketing a method of promoting products to customers

micro-encapsulation a process where particles of gas, liquids or solids are packaged within a polymer shell inside a fabric

microfibres very fine textile fibres, up to 60 times finer than a human hair, made primarily from polyester or nylon

modelling the developing and trying out of design ideas to see what works best; this can be done either using a computer or by making a model

modifications changes made to a product, usually to improve it

monochromatic colours that only contain the shades, tints and hues of one colour

monomers simple chemicals derived from oil or coal, which are joined together to make polymers

mordant a chemical used in dyeing that makes the dye permanent and helps prevent the colour leaking when cleaned or washed

non-conformance the additional costs incurred in producing faulty goods and the need for extra quality inspections, testing and the consequent reduced price of substandard goods

non-renewable materials that can never be renewed or re-created

one-off production when a product is made by one person, or only one is made

open questions questions included in a questionnaire which allow people to write in whatever answer they choose

organic shapes shapes that derive from living things

overlocker a machine that uses three or more threads at a time; it trims the seam and at the same time sews over the cut edge, enclosing the edges

pad or continuous dyeing a method of dyeing fabric where the fabric goes through a dye bath or through the dye pads and is squeezed through rollers to ensure even penetration of the dye

patchwork a technique for creating pattern or new fabric with leftover fabrics

pattern a 2D template that is used to make a 3D product

pattern technician a person with a very good knowledge of both design and construction of textiles products

permeable fabrics that allow water to pass through them

pill the formation of little bobbles on the surface of the fabric

pleats folds of fabric held in place by stitching along the fold edge

polymers a collection of monomers

pre-manufactured components components that are bought ready-made, such as Velcro and zip fasteners, to add to textiles products

primary recycling reusing textiles products in the same form as they were first produced

primary sources information which is gathered at first hand, for example questionnaires, surveys or shop visits.

process any step taken in the making of a product, such as adding pattern or colour to the fabric, sewing up the seams, or pressing the final product

product analysis a detailed examination of what other people have designed

product specification a detailed description of a particular product which is used by manufacturing companies to help make, as well as sell, their products

progressive bundle system a system of mass production where the bundles, which consist of all the pieces of the product, are sent along the production line

quality assurance the guarantee (assurance) to the customer that the product has been made to the highest possible standard from beginning to end

quality control a range of tests that are carried out on all parts of the product throughout manufacturing

quilting a process of sandwiching a soft cotton wool-like padding (batting) between two layers of fabric, then stitching through it to create a textured surface

resist a method of dyeing fabric where a coating, such as wax or a physical barrier such as string, are used to stop the dye being absorbed on certain areas of the fabric

risk assessment a careful examination of what could cause harm to people in the work area

satin stitch a series of stiches laid side by side, worked in close parallel lines to give a solid satin-like finish

seam a means of joining two pieces of fabric together

secondary recycling (physical recycling) recycling textiles products by changing and then reusing them

secondary sources information about a particular subject which has already been collected, for example in books and magazines

selvedge the edging of a fabric by the weft yarns wrapping round the warp yarns

semi-continuous dyeing a method of dyeing fabric where the fabric passes through the dye pads and is held on the roll at a given temperature for several hours

shirring elastic a type of elastic used in gathering, usually threaded onto the bobbin of a machine

shuttle loom a type of loom used to create simple plain weaves

single jersey plain knitted weft fabric

social responsibility documents documents used by many companies to detail their guidelines on environmental issues

stabilizer or interfacing material added to other fabrics, which helps to create a firm base for embroidery

standard sizing garment sizes produced from regular surveys of average measurements

staple short textile fibres found in wool and cotton

summative evaluation evaluation of a design that takes place at the end of all the processes included in the design work

system the means used to manage the way a product is produced

tertiary recycling (chemical recycling) recycling products by breaking them down and turning them into something else

texture one of the key principles of design. Texture describes what the surface of a product or fabric feels and looks like

thermosetting or thermoplastic the ability of fabrics to be manipulated using heat, which softens the fibres and allows the properties of the resulting fabric to be changed

tie dye a resist method of dyeing fabric, similar to tritik, but instead of sewing the fabric, it is wrapped, tied or folded in sections to stop the dye penetrating the fabric

time span duration or length of time taken

tritik a resist method of dyeing fabric, which uses stitching to prevent the dye reaching areas of the fabric

toile a model in paper or cheap fabric

tolerance the small amount of variance allowed on any process in manufacturing textiles products

toxicity how toxic a fabric is, for example when it is burned

tucks folds of fabric held in place by stitching where the folds join another piece of fabric

ultrasonic cutter a cutter used in industry to cut care labels from fabric; it gives a smooth soft edge to the label to avoid irritation to the user

warp yarn the yarns that lie vertically in the fabric

weaving a method of making fabric on a piece of equipment called a weaving loom

weft yarn the yarns that go horizontally across the fabric

wholesale price the price the retailer pays to the manufacturer for a product

work schedule a plan of the work to be done in manufacturing a product

Index